Australian
Poetry and Fiction

In the same series

Australian Literature and Indian Literature: Studies in Mutual Response
David Kerr and R.K. Dhawan, ed.

Australian Literature Today
R.K. Dhawan and David Kerr, ed.

A.D. Hope: Questions of Poetic Strength
Walter Tonetto

Australian
Poetry and Fiction

Edited by
R.K. Dhawan

PRESTIGE

Published by
Prestige Books
3/28, East Patel Nagar
New Delhi 110 008

ISBN: 81-7551-032-3

1997

Photo Typesetting by
Pivot Computers
Delhi 110 006

Printed at
Mehra Offset Press
New Delhi 110 002

Contents

Fiction

Australian Poetry and Fiction: An Introduction

R.K. DHAWAN

While several universities in Australia, including Melbourne, Adelaide, Wollongong, have a strong component of Indian English writing in their syllabi, there is an increasing interest in Australian writing amongst Indian scholars and several universities in India have started teaching this fast-growing area of study. A few years ago, scholars in Asia and elsewhere, seemed to be acquainted only with Patrick White, the only Nobel Prize winner Australian writer. He dominates the literary scene even today; he has become an object of serious and sustained study to such an extent that his work is regarded as the *sine qua non* of Australian literature courses. In the recent years, however, a number of Australian writers have emerged on the international literary scene. And these include Kenneth Slessor, A.D. Hope, Judith Wright, Les Murray, Chris Koch, Peter Carey, David Malouf, Elizabeth Jolley and a host of other writers.

II

Recently three eminent Australian creative writers visited India; they gave talks and read from their writings at various seminars and university centres. They were David Malouf, one of the best-known contemporary Australian novelists, and two women writers—Libby Hathorn and Gillian Mears. Penguin India organized their visits and also brought out their titles which were launched by the Australian Minister for Communications at India International Centre, New Delhi. Since I had the privilege of meeting and discussing with them various literary issues, I will like to introduce these writers to the readers. Broadly speaking, they are representative of the Australian writing today. While as David Malouf is a recognized novelist of repute, Libby Hathorn and Gillian Mears are promising, upcoming writers.

Gillian Mears, only thirty-two-years old, is considered one of the best new writers. Brought up in the coastal towns of New South Wales, she received a Bachelor of Arts degree in Communications from NSW Institute of Technology. Her short stories and poems have appeared frequently in Australian journals and magazines. She has been the recipient of several writing grants and short story prizes. She published her first collection of short stories *Ride a Cock Horse* in 1988; this collection won the South East Asian and South Pacific First Book Award. Her first novel *The Mint Lawn* won the prestigious Vogel Literary Award.

Mears, like Shashi Deshpande, writes mainly about women, and also about death of country towns in Australia. Her famous work *Fineflour* is her strongest statement on the latter. It is about recreating memory work and life lost in myth. The river Fineflour flows through the narrative as it flows through the township, linking time and space, character and event. The narrative follows lives that intermingle from one generation to the next. One of the stories in the collection, entitled "Welcome Home," is indeed fascinating. The female narrator and her daughter Lily are looking forward to receiving Rhys, at their home. There are intense moments of excitement and fear; Rhys is portrayed life-like, a round character, capable of surprising the readers. A notable feature of this work is that there are as many as three references to India in a brief story like this. Mears refers to (a) Indian *myna* (b) Indian silk cotton (c) the renowned guru Rajneesh. At one point in the story she explains a certain situation thus: "The one-legged *rajneeshee* growing an erection under his robe on the massage table." Mears has acquired this knowledge about India from the Indian community settled in Australia.

Mears' novel *The Mint Lawn* presents a dark account of a woman trapped both by her psychology and by her circumstances. Her writing is feminine, and as in the case of Shashi Deshpande, it creates fiction from the routine domestic experience. Her latest novel *Grass Sisters*, however, is about the immigrant experience and in that sense partakes the major concern of Bharati Mukherjee's fiction.

Libby Hathorn, another contemporary writer, is making a significant contribution to the literature for the young adults. She was born in New Castle, Australia. Several of her children's books have won awards; in 1992, she won the inaugural New South Wales Children's Week Award for her service to Children's literature.

Hathon's first novel for young adults *Thunderwith* is a classic Australian story that has won awards in Australia and Europe and was also named the Best Book for young adults in the United States. It relates the story of Lara who feels completely alone after the death of her mother. She is an intruder in her father's new family, living far away from all that has been familiar. It is indeed a powerful novel about hope and the human spirit's ability to finally win through.

David Malouf is internationally recognized as one of Australia's most gifted contemporary writers. His novels include *Johnno, The Great World, Harland's Half Acre, Fly Away Peter* and *Remembering Babylon.* He is the author of five collections, but it is essentially as a novelist that he is better known. He has won several international awards, including the Commonwealth Writers Prize for *The Great World* and the world's richest literary prize, the Dublin Literary Award for *Remembering Babylon.*

Malouf is well acquainted with the writing of Indian diaspora. He has not only read Salman Rushdie, Vikram Seth, Rohinton Mistry, Anita Desai, and V.S. Naipaul but has been nominated with them for a number of international literary awards. His novel *An Imaginary Life,* now available in Penguin India, is a work of unusual intelligence. The narrative strategy is skilful: the Roman poet Ovid, in exile, tells the story of his encounter with a wild boy, brought up among wolves in snow. At first, the poet assumes the role of a protector to the boy; gradually, however, the roles of protector and protected are reversed as the two form a curious and touching alliance.

In *An Imaginary Life* and his earlier works *Johnno* and *Fly Away Peter*, Malouf seems to reconcile his Australian experience with his European heritage. The impulse to bridge the two experiences comes from Malouf's own background, with his father's family coming to Brisbane from Lebanon in the 1880s, and his mother coming from middle-class Edwardian London of the early twentieth century.

III

The present volume reflects the literary response contemporary Australian poetry and fiction have evoked amongst scholars. In her article "Literature of Australia—The Land and Her People," Vinod Bala Sharma relates the geographical position and the natural distinctiveness of Australia to its art, its culture, the psyche of the people inhabiting it and their literary output. She refers to the work of Mary Gilmore and Walter Murdoch, Rex Ingamells and William Hartsmith, Watkin Trench and Henry Kendall, James Cuthbertson and Dorothea Mackeller in this context.

In her paper "Sociological and Historical Perspectives on Australia as Portrayed by Contemporary Australian Writers," Rosemary Kerr starts with the premise "History is not what happened but what is told" and "our view of reality is shaped by our view of History," and provides a glimpse of Australian society as shaped by a person's view of history.

She discusses in detail Robert Hughes' *The Fatal Shore*, Thomas Keneally's *Bring Larks and Heroes*, Kate Grenville's *Joan Makes History* and Eric Wilmot's *Pemulwuy: The Rainbow Warrior*.

Les Murray is one of the Australian poets who are busy in exploring the far recesses of their land and language. In his article "The Vernacular Republic: Les Murray's Poetic Transcription of Australian Popular Culture," Anurag Sharma presents Murray's poetic vision of future Australia—the Vernacular Republic as it emerges from his poems "The Returnees," "The Mitchells," "The Buladelah-Taree Holiday Song Cycle" and "The Commonwealth of Manu."

Love and death are the essential factors in every person's life. In her paper "Themes of Love and Death in the Poetry of Judith Wright and Sarojini Naidu," T. Bharathi attempts a comparative study of the various aspects of love presented by the two poets. There is sincerity and sensation in Judith Wright's love poetry. Sarojini Naidu's poetry too deals with sensuousness but there is no vulgar lust in it. Both of them express physical details of love making. Judith Wright's poems reflect on the continuity of creation and unity through love; Sarojini Naidu's love poetry sings of total devotion and surrender to the beloved.

Reluctant to plunge into the insubstantial and the fantastic romantic poetry, Judith Wright turns to the human world, riddled with problems of relationships and dehumanization. In "This is to Mourn a Man: Judith Wright's 'Interface I,' 'Interface II' and 'Interface III,'" Madhumalati Adhikari argues that Judith Wright narrates in these poems not the whale's story but the story of mankind through the ages. The concept of "Interface" used as a metaphor interprets human life through the analogy of a whale story.

Urbashi Barat, in her article "Judith Wright and the White Goddess: A View of 'Fourth Quarter' and 'Easter Moon and Owl,'" takes up another aspect of Judith Wright's poetry—the relation between femininity and creativity. Woman is fertile, waving and waning in her monthly cycle, part of the generative processes of the earth. Above all, she is the symbol of the instincts and the passion, the ruler of the night and the unconscious, and the source and the inspirer of poetry. Judith Wright's "Fourth Quarter" is an assertion of the undying human spirit of creativity that will not be stilled even though the body itself may fail. In "Easter Moon and Owl," the relationship between femininity and poetic creativity is examined through its exploration of the mythical kinship between the White Goddess and the woman-poet.

In his brilliant article "The Changing Face of Australian Literature: Some Multi-Cultural Novels," Ron Shapiro, whose parents reached Australia from Britain in 1949, takes up for discussion three multi-cultural novels, namely *The Time of the Peacock* by Mena Abdullah, *Seasonal Adjustments* by Adib Khan and *The Ganges and its Tributaries* by Christopher Cyrill. The three novels have a common "Indian" theme: the migrants in each novel are expected not just to integrate into Australian society but to assimilate, that is, to become like white Australians.

Nations are defined by their boundaries, but these boundaries join as well as separate. In his "Nations without States: The Search for Home in H.H. Richardson's *Fortunes of Richard Mahony* and Yasmine Gooneratne's *A Change of Skies*," John McLaren takes up for detailed discussion two novels published at the either end of the twentieth century, dealing with the cultural conflicts of the first and the latest waves of migration. The migrants in Richardson's trilogy and Gooneratne's novel are displaced from island colonies, Ireland and Sri Lanka respectively, yet carry with them a wider sense of nationality based on imperial loyalties to an idealized island of Great Britain. The image that connects the two novels is the change of skies.

A.G. Khan's "Bushes in Two Hemispheres: A Comparative Study of Susanna Moodie's *Roughing it in the Bush* and Yasmine Gooneratne's *A Change of Skies*" studies human predicament in two different hemispheres of people caught in adverse circumstances. Both the novels are autobiographies. While Susanna Moodie's novel has sketches of people and accounts of events, Gooneratne's novel is a post-modernist work comprising biography, autobiography and newspaper reports.

My Brilliant Career by Miles Franklin is a bildungsroman concerned with maturation and education of the heroine Sybylla Penelope Melvin. Madhuri Chatterjee's article "Miles Franklin's *My Brilliant Career*: A Feminist Perspective" deals with Sybylla's initiation into the patriarchal world, her conflict and finally her self-discovery. She concludes by saying, "In a long tradition of women's writing, *My Brilliant Career* is a text which has successfully attempted to raise many feminine statements."

Elizabeth Jolley is one of the best known women writers of Australia. She has published poetry in anthologies and journals, three collections of short fiction and nine novels. K. Radha points out in her paper "Humour in Elizabeth Jolley's *My Father's Moon*" that the novel is full of humour even though the theme is pathetic. She singles out a number of incidents which contribute to the humour and at times to the irony in the novel.

Postcolonial writing in Australia, Canada, New Zealand and the United States has differed from its counterparts elsewhere. In Australia in particular, the theme of entrapment or imprisonment—reflecting white Australia's origins as a penal colony—has been a major theme. In "The Theme of Entrapment in Peter Carey's Fiction," M.D. Fletcher looks at some of the ways in which the theme of entrapment or imprisonment is deployed by Peter Carey in his three novels, namely *Bliss, Illywhacker*, and *Oscar and Lucinda.* In "Parodying the Picaresque in Peter Carey's *Illywhacker*," M.D. Fletcher reads *IllyWhacker* as a parody of the picaresque form, as part of a broader postcolonial writing.

Patrick White belongs to the great tradition of novelists like F. Dostoevsky, Leo Tolstoy, D.H. Lawrence and James Joyce and has achieved world-wide recognition for his novels. Four articles in the present anthology are devoted to his writing. Shaik Samad's "Mandala Symbolism in the Novels of Patrick White" argues that the mandala image is central to an understanding of the religious vision of Patrick White. It traces the mandala symbolism in all White's novels—*The Living and the Dead, The Aunt's Story, The Tree of Man, Voss, Riders in the Sea, The Solid Mandala, The Vivisector, The Eye of the Storm, A Fringe of Leaves* and *The Twyborn Affair.* D.N. Bandyopadhyay in his "Text and Meaning: A Deconstructive Analysis of Patrick White's *Voss*" and V.C. Sudheer in his "Indomitable Spirit of Nature in *Voss*" deal with the adventures of Voss who attempts to overreach the untoward circumstances of life by trying to cross the Australian continent for the first time. In her brillianat paper "A New Passage to India: Patrick White's *The Tree of Man*," Veronica Brady analyzes the novel most in tune with traditional Indian culture. She concludes by saying, "*The Tree of Man* opens the way to a deeper rapprochement between Australia and India."

Pradeep Trikha's "Australian Short Fiction: The Last Thirty Years" presents a survey of the short story writing in the last three decades. It discusses the significant contribution made by Michael Wilding, Frank Moorhouse, Peter Carey, Murray Bail, Robert Dawe and others to this genre. C.L.L. Jayaprada's "Sense of Place in the Short Stories of Barbara Baynton" takes up for detailed discussion the presentation of the bush life in a number of stories by Barbara Baynton.

The papers collected in this volume give critical responses to the contemporary Australian poetry and fiction, enhancing our understanding and knowledge in this area.

Literature of Australia—The Land and Her People

VINOD BALA SHARMA

The greatest literature is the one which is universal and yet all great literature is local in the sense that it is based on a certain culture and all great culture is conditioned on the environmental values of the place where the writer belongs. The geographical position and the natural distinctiveness of a country is a fact, too fundamental to be ignored while assessing and appreciating its art, its culture, the psyche of the people inhabiting it and their literary output. The same is true of Australian literature, the natural distinctiveness of the Australian continent is axiomatic in the history of this Continent, its bearing on the people who inhabited it either as natives or as migrants is self-evident.

"Australian culture is at present in a nebulous stage," wrote Rex Ingamells. He along with many others felt that the Australian writers had not arrived at a clear view of the distinctiveness of their country. The preoccupation with questions of national identity and culture had started as early as the eighteenth century. The foundation of the "Bulletin" in Sydney in 1880 established the nationalist movement which lasted until after the second world war and still exercises a certain influence, though not all Australian writers of the modern period can be fitted in it.

To consider the writers collectively and individually, we must consider, first, some aspects of Australia. I start with a passage from Mary Gilmore which can be taken as a representative poem. Showing the Australians's great adoration for her landscape. "Even in my own life she was a scented land. In spring the bush used to be a constant choir of song. Wings were everywhere, throughout the changing years might be heard continual flying of birds: curlews, plovers, travelling duck, swans, wandering owls, bitterns, night-jars, and in the swamp the bleat of the snipe. . . . The Almighty had poured out for plenty, and the blackman had guarded that plenty by his care for balance."

There is in the writings of Mary Gilmore nostalgia for the simplicities of the past and a sense of injury at the encroachment by the

English, "There were no bad smells about the bush when the Kingdom of the Wild was its own Kingdom . . . it was not till the settlement came that the earth stank, and sewers burst. Once Australia smelt like Spice-Islands. . . . Ships knew before they came to her, 'We are near Australia,' said the seamen, 'can't you smell the flowers?'" The settlers who came were blind to its beauty—they were not only apathetic but even malicious. Gilmore complains that the land of flowers had been sullied by the "thick nosed and dull-eared" who derided it. They called her a land of songless birds and scentless flowers: "She was a scented land and we were taught to look otherwise, . . . And she was a scented land. . . . And only the exile knew her."

"As the exile knew her" is significant. According to most of the Australian writers only those who were born in Australia and partially the first fleeters saw the unspoilt, untarnished beauty of the place. The first fleeters saw, only the abundance of this beauty, only those who were born in Australia could partake in its indestructible power. There were great writers, D.H. Lawrence, for example, who tried too capture the spirit of her beauty, but he too failed to realize if fully. Rex Ingamells says of Lawrence, "he did not feel at home in the bush, although its power gripped him. D.H. Lawrence may have written a superb piece of natural description at the beginning of Kangaroo but he could never feel like thousands of Australians do, with childlike devotion the familiar beauty and utter loneliness of the outback environment in many of its moods . . . they have only not found an eloquent tongue to express it."

Of the earnest devotion and patriotism of these writers there can be no question. There are, according to Walter Murdoch, more than three hundred odes to Western Australia, by poets like him, who have experienced the beauty and magnificence of her landscape and have felt enthralled even by its grimmer side. Of this grimmer side there could be no better example than Murdoch's description of a fire in "The Valley." "No language could convey an idea of the wonder and terror and beauty of the spectacle by night, when the valley below you and the hill-sides around you are all one red roaring hell of furious destruction . . . the flying flame, the growling and crackling and blustering, the loose-barked trees on fire from top to toe, and scattering with every gust of wind a shower of burning leaves and the crashing of a falling giant."

The second important factor that has influenced Australian literature most, as we all know, is the feeling for the Aboriginal. There were devotees of the Aboriginal culture, sympathizers and promoters, writers who proclaimed the right of the Aboriginal and started a movement forwarding his cause, which culminated in the Jindyworobak School in the late thirties. There were others who found the Aboriginal revulsive and were drawn by a sense of repugnance and still others who looked at them with an impartial eye, studying them as a historian or anthropologist would do.

The poets of the Jindyworobak School emphasized the importance of the Aboriginal culture and poets like Rex Ingamells and William Hartsmith worked to promote literature having roots in the Aboriginal culture. Ingamells paints a panorama of the Australian circumstance in the poem "History of the Ships Bringing the Convicts":

> Pioneer ships lumbering in the sunset
> Lumbering along our sombre eastern coastline
> Swaying, awkward but beautiful, north to Port Jackson

and then the convicts

> The stark hatred and reeking soul-fire of men's faces . . .
> herded as cattle, worked as cattle

and the Immigrants

> Stern-hearted free-men, felling tall trees, building
> rough home-steads, amid far, unfamiliar places,
> hoping, cherishing, their pre-conceived
> visions of beauty and propriety

and the plight of the natives struggling to survive

> Bones of cattle, camels, horses, men
> And the despised black who lives through it all,
> finding himself water, native plums, yams
> and wild-honey from honey-ants . . .

For a fair assessment of the Englishman's attitude towards the native, we must begin with the earliest settlers. The more interesting writing of the early years of settlement is mainly in the form of letters, diaries, memoirs, journals and reports and is not strictly literary in intention. In these writings there is a recurring preoccupation with hardships of the early settlements, differences in the Antipodes, England and Australia, sense of distance and isolation, mysteries of the unexplored regions and excitement of discovery and hopes for the future.

Watkin Trench an Englishman who was in Australia from 1788 to

1792 writes of the natives with a clemency and understanding which other migrants do not seem to have shared. Trench was not surprised that the natives failed to understand what motives could induce these Englishmen to encounter, labour, fatigue and pain, when they might remain in repose at home, "all savages hated toil and placed happiness in inaction" says an early writer of them. In contrast to the adventurous English, they resisted everything that involved risk. The writer is, however, impressed by their physical superiority, as they walked stoutly, appeared but little fatigued and maintained their spirits admirably, laughing to excess when any of us either tripped or stumbled.

A contemporary of Watkin Trench has, however, a different picture to paint. The whole place, is, to Marcus Clarke full of forebodings. "The Australian mountain forests are funeral—Hopeless explores have named them out of their sufferings. Mount Misery, Mount Dreadful, Mount despair." From a corner of the silent forest rises a dismal chant, and around a fire dance natives painted like skeletons. All is fear-inspiring and gloomy. To the native poet, the very same mountains became sacred and sanctimonious, the messengers of holy thoughts. Henry Kendall in his dedication to a mountain hears god's great authentic gospel while kneeling to a mountain.

The song is that of the Bush, the Bush that the Australian has loved, the foreigner traversed, admired or halied but never loved. The Australian loves to be in the lap of his country and wishes that the trespassers would leave it alone. James Lisler Cuthbertson echoes the same sentiment when he asks:

> give us from dawn to dark
> Blue of Australian skies
> Let there be none to mark
> Whither our pathway lies.

and Dorothea Mackeller speaks of her country as

> An opal-hearted country
> A wilful, lavish land
> All you who have not loved her
> You will not understand—
> Though earth holds many splendours
> Wherever I may die
> I know to what brown country
> My homing thoughts will fly.

Sociological and Historical Perspectives on Australia as Portrayed by Contemporary Australian Writers

ROSEMARY KERR

Working from the premise "History is not what happened but what is told" and "our view of reality is shaped by our view of History" and by using my own interpretation of Realist literature, I had to provide a glimpse of Australian society as shaped by a person's view of history. My field is not literature, not social work and definitely not the world of the academic. My field is not literature, not social work and definitely not the world of the academic; my field is education. One of my major vices is curiosity and this linked with enthusiasm leads me to a very adaptive style and approach to education.

I would like to introduce some of you to Australian writers you may not know about, and, to those of you who have broad knowledge of Australian literature I hope to give a sociological view. I intend to use the term literature in its broadest of terms. I am going to use it to encompass all forms of the written word from literary works of fiction and non-fiction. In this sense I am going to deal with my own view of Realist literature. I see Realist literature in the following way:

1. "Facts" incorporated in fiction
2. "Facts" exagerated in fiction
3. "Facts" that conflict with the official record
4. Non-fiction written to convey facts.

I ask myself: "is the realist style in literature an imitation of reality?"

The well-known Australian writer David Malouf says: "History is not what happened but what we are told." The literature I am going to put before you will give you a surface knowledge of the sociological and historical events that have contributed to social attitudes and conditions in Australia today. It should help you understand the white Australian's view of himself and also conditions that black Australians wish to change in order to regain their own lost dignity.

The first piece of literature to be mentioned is a work of non-fiction by Robert Hughes, *The Fatal Shore*. This book has been widely acclaimed in Australia and has won at least one major prize. For those of you who teach Australian colonial literature it would be an invaluable tool for presenting and understanding the background to the material you may choose to study. It is readily available in both hard and soft cover.

Hughes researched a number of official and private documents and his work gives a vivid account of how 160,000 men, women and children, some innocent, some not, were shipped off the face of the known world. The late Georgian and early Victorian authorities in England seemed to have but one aim in mind, this being to eventually remove a whole class of people—the "criminal class"—from British shores.

Like Robert Hughes, I grew up with "as skimpy sense of Colonial Australia. Convict history was ignored in schools and little taught in universities—indeed, the idea that the convicts might have a history worth-telling was foreign to Australians in the 1950s and 1960s."

My own introduction to colonial Australia came from a creative history teacher when I was in year 8. She chose to introduce an aspect of our history through reading Henry Lawson's powerful and moving stories of the settlers's life and hardships, its loneliness and despair graphically portrayed in "Water them geraniums" and "Past Cavin." My imagination and emotions were immediately involved and I was "hooked" on Australian colonial history and on Lawson.

The inescapable fact is: "Never had a colony been founded so far from its parent state; or in such ignorance of the land it occupied. There had been no reconnaisance. In 1770 Captain James Cook had made land fall on the unexplored east coast of his utterly enigmatic continent, stopped for a short time at a place called Botany Bay and gone north again. Since then no ship had called: not a word, not an observation, for seventeen years, each one of which was exactly like the thousands that had preceded it, looked in its historical immensity of blue heat, bush, sandstone and the measured booming of glossy Pacific rollers." In this factual prose, Hughes manages to convey the isolation and alien environment in which the settlement was established, and contrast it with a sense of timeless beauty still to be experienced by Australians today on our Eastern coastline. Hughes goes on to describe the flora and fauna so unfamiliar to the English and Irish convicts. He states the only predator experienced in the environment as being man.

The work I choose to look at next is the work of a well-known novelist and Booker prize winner Thomas Keneally. The novel being *Bring Larks and Heroes.* I believe Keneally exaggerated some facts in this novel to make history more powerful. In doing so he has raised the consciousness of the reader and brought home with force the brutality and suffering of many white Australian's ancestors.

Barry Andrews, in his article "More sinned against than sinning: A note on the convict legend," states that the convicts in their own narrative representation of convict life, often distorted the facts by: (a) making an exaggeration of their own innocence, (b) emphasizing the brutality of the system to strengthen the cautionary tale they told, (c) by keeping in mind and writing to the audience in the British Isles who further represented in their own folksong and street literature, the image of the convict beset by tribulation and oppression.

The brutality, as witnessed in humanitarian writing, is true. However the brutalness of both sides was often played down in official records so as not to frighten off prospective free settlers.

The horrors did happen but not to every convict. There is evidence that four and a half tons of convict records were burnt in 1863. In 1871 Marcus Clarke wrote of massive destruction of records in Tasmania. Even as late as 1901 the following question was asked in parliament:

Mr. Darcy: I wish to ask the Colonial Secretary whether it is a fact that the person editing the public records in New South Wales has power to suppress whatever he deems right?

Mr. Sec: I am not aware of the fact, but I will cause enquiries to be made. After all, perhaps there are some matters in connection with the history of New South Wales which it is just as well not to perpetuate. I know that the late Sir John Robertson ordered the destruction of old records.

Robert Hughes claims, *Bring Larks and Heroes* is "the best thing to come out of Australia since Patrick White's *Riders in the Chariot,*" and Leonie Kramer states, "only a writer of unusual talent would succeed in making so moving a parable out of our heritage of cruelty."

Keneally, being an ex-seminarian, has drawn not only from, and I believe exaggerated, official records but he has also drawn on his own knowledge of religious faith and superstitions prevalent in the eighteenth and nineteenth centuries. One finds many references to Irish Catholicism. He mentions the cord worn around the waist beneath the clothes of Irish women in the belief that it would prevent pregnancy and refers to a situation as "smelling like a cemetery after *All Souls Day.*" Keneally cannot resist moralizing. A classic example being when Mrs. Blythe says to Corporal Halloran: "The pledges of men of affairs have given us the appearance of a godly nation. The breaking of those pledges have given us an Empire."

Keneally describes a situation when the hero of the novel is sent to collect a convict from an outpost. When he arrives, Halloran is told: "You can't have him. His backs gone rotten." Later he writes: "Drowned in the stench, he forgot it for seconds at a time. The long room sizzled with the consequential gluttony of flies, and that too he no longer averted to. But to see in an instant and by surprise, a scam in the boy's back and a herd of black flies, where bite is maggots, drinking from it, that made him flee." We later discover this badly maltreated conduct was suspected of subversive activitives. He was taken out and lashed in an attempt to make him talk. He had not been charged with any offence nor had the incident of the lashing been recorded.

I suggest, by writing so graphically of the brutality, and describing people as having been given 500 lashes—a thrashing I feel nobody could possibly survive—Keneally has raised our consciousness by exaggerating facts. This exaggeration helps many Australians take pride instead of shame, in the so-called convict origins.

David Malouf says in an interview with Candida Baker: "People actually live their lives according to the conventions that fiction has created in our culture since the eighteenth century, and our view of reality is shaped of course by what we see as the shape of history."

Keneally is one of our best-known novelists and would be a good choice for study by members of another culture. There are a wide variety of articles about his work to further discussion and understanding.

I would now like to move away from Keneally but I still wish to keep before you David Malouf's contention that our view of reality is shaped by our view of history.

The Australian view of reality has been shaped by the view that the country's history began with white settlement. We are given the view the British arrived in an empty land. This of course is not so.

Before proceeding further I wish to make clear my terminology. I will refer to the Australian Aboriginal as a black. This is the term preferred by them when being spoken of collectively.

Apart from the individual tribal name, a number of tribal groups in a particular area were referred to as either Murries (Queensland) Koories, Nimbans, Noongas and so on. There is no one word that encompasses the entire black population. Hence when I use the term "blacks" I am not being racist but using the desired term.

Robert Hughes refers to a common view of black culture still seen in the eyes of white city dwellers as "A static culture, frozen by its immemorial primitivism, unchanged in an unchanging landscape." He also refers to further "myths about the Noble Savage, misreadings of aboriginal technology, traditional racism and ignorance of Australian prehistory" as contributing to this common view which I am happy to say is slowly changing.

Archaelogical findings prove that the blacks were roaming Australia for at least 40,000 years before the British arrived. The blacks believe that they have always been there. When the first fleet arrived, there were perhaps 300,000 blacks in the whole of Australia. They were living a nomadic life. They were not agrarian in any way. They lived off the land from day to day. "They had no notion of private property but they were intensely territorial, linked to the ancestral area by hunting customs and totemism. Hundreds of tribes existed at the time of white invasion. . . . The tribe did not have a king, or a charismatic leader, or even a formal council. It was linked together by a common religion, by language and by an intricate web of family relationships; it had no writing, but instead a complex structure of spoken and sung myth whose aroma were gradually passed on by elders to the younger men."

"There is ample evidence to show the British interpretation of them as ignorant, neglectful and subhuman, to be quite incorrect." They were a shrewd sensible race building no shelter when such things as caves existed for them to live in and using all kinds of cunning tricks to catch game for food. Their culture was simple and effective. However, seen through white Georgian eyes they failed the measure set for a conventional cultural view.

Kate Grenville writes of the attitude of the new settlers in her novel *Joan Makes History*:

> Civilization was fine stone houses with lions and sundials, it was legs of mutton and tumblers of rum and water, and it was solid fences that left no doubt at all about ownership. All day the valley was filled with the hollow knock of axes against wood as another bit of post-and-rail went up around another square of dirt: a fence gave a man like Burchett the courage to puff himself up and become righteous about thieves and robbers.
>
> By whom he chiefly meant the blacks, of course: the blacks who came to the kitchen door from time to time, grinning in their saucy way and cadging a bit of sugar of tea or flour, exotic delicacies to them. They did not understand about fences, or owning things, and they did not have to labour mightily with hoes to extract a bit of nourishment from the soil. (125)
>
> What did they find here to eat, those skinny black folk, in these empty-looking hillsides of nothing in particular? What were they feeding on in the nights, that made them laugh so much? (125)
>
> If a sheep was found killed and thrown on one of their fires, or if a blanket went missing, Burchett grew purple with outrage, and

> small bands of men went up into the hillsides with guns over their shoulders and retribution on their minds. (124)

On one occasion when the central character of this novel was walking in the bush she discovers a black woman who is very ill. The situation and its cause are described thus:

> what I found as I blundered and marvelled was a person, dark brown, naked, wild of eye, female, in anguish.
>
> She had known I was there long before I had seen her, and gave me no more than a rolling white-eyed glance from her streaming face as she hunched over herself, keening among the ferns and the trickling water. I stopped short, feeling my skirt fanned out behind me, trapped on some thorn or other, and felt my lunch rise bile-like into my throat as I watched this metallic female coil over herself and retch, choking and bringing up long threads of yellow spit. She held her belly with both hands, hugging it, stilling it, crying in pain and something worse, grief and loss, and fell to her knees, still embracing her round brown belly. Then I saw that the gleam and shine on her thighs was not just the polished gleam of her skin, but liquid of the thick kind. I saw now that it could only be thick painful blood, oozing out from between her thin legs and streaming down the skin, although with trembling horrified hands, wailing, she tried to keep inside her what was determined to come out. . . .
>
> *It is all right*, I said and kept saying as I approached her. *Do not despair, and God is with you and will grant you another*. It comforted me to know that she could not understand the words, so I did not have to try to get them right, I needed only to speak to her fear and pain, of others near, of sympathy, of the caring of one stranger for another in travail. (128-29)

Joan returns to the house to find:

> what was happening was stranger even than Burchett crying: it was Burchett laughing, and I saw too that Madam's hard face was also broken up, in a way that was frightening, by mirth.
>
> I felt fear then, because Burchett and his Madam would laugh only out of some wickedness done, and I knew that I would not be laughing with them if I knew what they were finding so funny. I was chilled as I crossed the room through their hideous humour, hearing Burchett say: *See the way they were grinning away, too*

> *stupid and savage to know any better.* Madam laughed a raucous laugh like a cockatoo triumphant over a grub in a tree, and shouted in her hilarity: *And didn't they think they was that clever, lifting it from under our very noses*! Chill prickled and goosefleshed me then and I could not leave the room quickly enough, stifled by the possibility of understanding what it was they found so funny.
>
> But out in the cold kitchen, where Sid sat, as I had known, smoking his hands like small hams at the smoulder in the hearth, it was no better, for Sid was gabbing to dull Will, and I was forced to bustle over pease and pork so that I could not escape to anywhere else. No matter what a clattering and banging I produced with pots and pans and iron spoons, I could not help hearing Sid telling Will what I did not want to hear: *Them dumb blacks*, Sid shouted, and Will grinned and goggled. *Three bags they made off with, plenty for all them thieving heathens to go to Kingdom Come and back!*
>
> I could not eat the vile food I cooked that night, could not even make a pannikin of tea go down my throat, clenched tight against the images in my mind's eye. They were all in fine fettle, though, those other human beings I shared my life with, and gorged themselves, knowing the plenty of summer was coming, even Burchett cramming great forkfuls of pork into his mouth until the grease ran down his chin. They ate, and gulped at their tea, and were full of joy, knowing that out among those tiny lascivious flowers, under bushes full of thorns, in gullies of trembling ferns, that woman and her tribe, whose wallabies had made the saliva gush into our mouths, were in agony, with their bellies full of damper poisoned with our hatred and fear.

The cultural view and ignorance of the Australian blacks caused many such reactions.

Kate Grenville is a fairly new Australian writer with only two or three works of fiction published. To my knowledge no criticism of her work is available as yet.

I am not trying to paint a picture of the Australian black as a harmless innocent. They had many customs we from our culture would find repugnant. I am merely trying to redress the balance. The feminist movement would be appalled at their attitude to women. They were seen as mere chattels. Warriors, before setting off on a revenge mission against some other group, would swap their women as a mark of brotherhood. If a tribal group was about to be attacked and knew where its enemies were, it would sometimes send out a party of women in their direction; the attackers would then show they were open to a peaceful solution by copulating with them. But if the women came back untouched, it was a signal that there was no choice but battle.

A much written about member of the lora tribe was a black named Bennelong. He was the first black to learn English, drink rum, wear clothes and eat the invaders's food. He went to England in 1792 with Governor Phillip. In 1795 he returned to Australia. Bennelong became increasingly sodden and pugnacious with rum and died at the age of forty in 1813. This fate is the most common for the Australian black today.

There was however another lesser known native of prominence in the lora tribe. His name was Pemulwuy. There is no doubt of his existence or of the problems he caused for the British. Governor Philip Gidley King wrote of him in 1802: "He was a brave and independent character." The legend of Pemulwuy is part of the belief system and oral history of the black people of the east coast of Australians. The city of Sydney is built upon his land. He led the lora people in the first major response to the British invasion, and fought the British for twelve long years until his death in 1802. Until recently, his name never appeared in any white Australian history, yet he lives on in the unpublished records of his enemies, and in the minds of black Australians.

The name Pemulwuy means: man of the earth. He was born around 1756 to a people who believed their world was brought into being by the temporal form of the rainbow. He was the rainbow warrior. It is around this character that Eric Wilmot has chosen to write his novel: *Pemulwuy: The Rainbow Warrior.* He has used oral history which has now become legend and Pemulwuy assumes the aura of supernatural powers. He has also used now published government records of the time.

The novel points up the aboriginal belief that no one can own the land. The land does not belong to people, the people belong to the land. This gives enlightenment to Robert Hughes's statement of tribes being very territorial. If a black cannot be put to rest on the land on which he was born he believes his spirit will wander the country in torment. This explains the on-going battle for "Land Rights" that exists between the blacks and white Australians.

Eric Wilmot has constructed his novel around another basic black belief called: The three parts of truth. The first part of truth is what is seen to be. The second part of truth is the truth in other people's minds, and the third and final part of truth, which in Pemulwuy's case is not revealed until the end of the novel is: "The secret truth within each person, namely our fate and for destiny." Pemulwuy becomes an almost Christ-like figure. As the novel progresses he desperately tries to unite his people in direct opposition to the invaders, encouraging them in ferocious and cunning fighting. He wins many battles but is ultimately forced to foresee his people's defeat due to the superior weaponry of the British. When he realizes the futility of the fight he also realizes his own third part of truth. He then proceeds to meet it:

> Some seven days after this meeting, Kiraban and Pemulwuy were dead, caught by the constabulary in an ambush that even Boolayoo could have avoided. Kiraban was killed by a single musket shot; for Pemulwuy, death was not so easy. He fell to the ground with four musket balls in his body. As he lay living in his own blood, a man moved purposefully from among the British ranks.
>
> "We must be sure!" he said.
>
> With swift, merciless movements of a sabre, Pemulwuy's head was struck from his body.

To help understand the attitude of the Australian black, personified in the novel by Pemulwuy, I refer you to a poem by Tagore: "A Half-acre of Land."

> I had forfeited all my land except for one half-acre.
> The landlord said, 'Upen, I'll buy it, you must hand it over.'
> I said, 'You're rich, you've endless land, can't you see
> That all I've got is a patch on which to die?'
> 'Old man,' he sneered, 'you know I've made a garden,
> If I have your half-acre its length and breadth will be even.
> You'll have to sell.' Then I said with my hands on my heart
> And tears in my eyes, 'Don't take my only plot!
> It's more than gold—for seven generations my family.
> Has owned it: must I sell my own mother through poverty?'
> He was silent for a while as his eyes grew red with fury
> 'All right, we'll see,' he said smiling cruelly.

This poem as you know goes on to tell of the man losing the land and wandering for many years and then returning to be accused of being a thief and a robber. The same is happening to the Australian black. The last scene in *Pemulwuy* is of a soldier telling Bennelong of Pemulwuy's death. The last line is: "Pemulwuy is dead. It is over."

Armed resistance did not work. Assimilation did not work. But as Pemulwuy implied you can only lose a war if you fight violently. The last line of the novel is historically untrue. *It is not over.* One only has to read the daily newspapers to know the black battle is not over. It seems it is only just beginning and all forms of realist literature are raising the world's consciousness.

The Vernacular Republic: Les Murray's Poetic Transcription of Australian Popular Culture

ANURAG SHARMA

It has been widely acknowledged that Murray is one of those handful of poets writing in English today who are devoutly busy in exploring the far recesses of their land and language. This gigantic task demands the epical performance of a genius as it involves a creativity of a high imaginative order and also perceptive ability to discover a meaning in the phenomena of life. After all, to be the spokesman of a vast segment of people, to be the voice of a nation is not that easy. Murray has taken upon himself the task to name and define what he himself means and also what others have meant by 'Australia' and 'Australianness.'

Quite early in his career as a poet, Murray seemed to be aware of the issues facing the present-day Australian society and defined his preoccupations and ideology based on the concept of convergence. He has always been for the convergence of cultures—urban, rural and Aboriginal—in Australia. It is here that he associates himself with the Jindyworobak movement, the poets of which were for the assimilation of two cultures—urban and Aboriginal. For Murray, however "convergence is a better word here, though: assimilation carried too deep a stain of conquest, of expecting the Aborigines to make all the accommodations while white people make none."[1]

Readers of Murray's poetry are attracted by the coherence of the thematic concerns that appear and reappear quite frequently and consistently in his poems and prose-pieces. He has dealt with these concerns in the following way: "Western man must rediscover a core of religious values and recover certain traditional modes of being; society should embrace a more democratic equalitarianism, avoiding the twin perils of eliticism and false ideology; aboriginal attitudes regarding nature and the environment need to be better understood by white Australians and to some extent adopted; Australia itself represents an island of hope in the world, as a place where many of the divisive features undermining modern society might be finally reconciled."[2]

Murray has his own poetic vision of future Australia—it would be Vernacular Republic. This Vernacular Republic with the Boeotian values of life—with ceremony and custom, cattle-place and green pastures, religion and poetry—is something that we Indians have inherited from our forefathers. He is the poet of Australia in a way Tagore is of India. Ken Goodwin says: "In Murray's view, the nation of Australia, its landscape and rural industries, its communities, its beliefs and its literature should all share certain qualities, the qualities that he metonymically describes as Boeotian. These values are rural, even provincial, directly related to the land; concerned with religion and its ritual rather than with the abstractions of philosophy; based on the family rather than the political unit, and egalitarian rather than rigidly democratic."[3]

Murray's poetry presents the convergence of not only three cultures prevalent at present but also of three Australias: the one that physically speaking, is no more but whose shadows implicitly affect the contemporary life patterns; secondly, the Australia of the post-industrial world with extreme industrialization and a boom of money-making culture and the eroding traditional fibres of Australian society; and finally, the future Australia of Murray's dreams, the natural; outgrowth of all that has been and gone by. Murray wishes "to see Australians escaping . . . not towards the past, but towards futures which have no existence until we discover and settle them, for our own good and the whole life of mankind."[4] Murray finds this vision of his Vernacular Republic, "inherent in our folk tradition, which is to say in that 'folk' Australia, part imaginary and part historical, which is the real matrix of any distinctiveness we possess as a nation, and which stands over against all of our establishments and colonial elites. This is the Australia of our deepest common values and identifications, the place of our quiddities and priorities and family jokes. . . . It [the Vernacular Republic] is the subsoil of our common life and to live consciously outside it, or in opposition to it without expatriating oneself is a cripping strain."[5]

No wonder, Murray has been very aptly called the Whitman of Australia: "Like Whitman . . . Murray is unashamedly democratic, anticolonial and assertively, often aggressively, local."[6] In his discussion with Peter Porter, Murray has called the Australian way of life and arts as Boeotian. Murray's Boeotians "prefer dance, pageant, sport, religion and precept."[7] For Murray, Peter Porter represented the Attic values as opposed to his own Boeotian ones. He was quite firm in his opinion that "Australians must not succumb to European socialist *misere;* they must recognize the chance given by a new land to embrace happiness. The best way to promote happiness nationally is to be ritualized, but the ritual must include the whole people."[8]

The Murrayesque notion of the Vernacular Republic inculcating the participation of the whole people in a sort of ritualized happiness is equivalent to what is defined as popular culture by the *Fontana Dictionary of Modern Thought*. It says: "Historically, popular culture refers to the oral, folk or little 'traditon' of the pre-literate mass; this vernacular cultural tradition is usually distinguished from the more esoteric high or 'great' culture characterized by its association with objects, texts and scores that are accessible through an extended and developed sense of Aesthetics. . . . Popular culture has . . . become understood in terms of active processes and practices as well as objects and artifacts and encompasses a variety of phenomena including mail order catalogues, the design of cars and other consumer durables."[9] This popular culture "includes rituals, activities, the 'way of life' of a popular people in a particular culture,"[10] says McGregor. He also quotes Bigsby who in his book *Approaches to Popular Culture* points out, "popular culture is . . . a vital rediscovery of a dimension of human existence formerly denied not so much by technology . . . but by a persistent puritanism and a bourgeois power structure."[11] The following analysis of some poems of Murray will justify the points already referred to in the foregoing discussion.

In the poem, "The Returnees," Murray describes a typical scene of social or ritualized happiness in the Australian countryside. "The poem speaks of those feelings and belief which bring men together."[12] The poet describes in the poem how some friends rowing in a lake happen to see a snake swimming head-high, in the water.

> As we were rowing to the lakes
> our oars were blunt and steady wings
> the tanbark-coloured water was a
> gruel of pollen: more coming down
> hinted strange futures to our cells
> the far hills ancient under it
> the corn flats black-green under beat
> were cut in an antique grainy gold
>
> it was the light of Boeotian art.[13] (105)

The whole scene is full of sharp contrasts. "Tanbark-coloured water" is a "gruel of pollen"; "strange futures" are silhoutted against the "far" ancient "hills" and the black-green "corn flats" glare out like "an antique grainy gold." By defining this Australian landscape as "Boeotian," the poet has given it a root—not mythological but historical. This

"Boeotian art" is called "unsnubbing art" in the second section which may be regarded as a symphony of sounds, typically Australian.

> Bestowing tourbillons that drowned
> the dusty light we had used up
> pulling the distance to us, we
> were conscious of a lifelong sound.
>
> On everything, that low fly-humming
> melismatic untedious endless.
> Note that a drone-pipe-plus-chants or
>
> (shielding our eyes, rocking the river)
>
> A ballad—some ballads—catch, the one
> some paintings and many yarners summon
> the ground-note of unsnubbing art
>
> cicadas were in it, and that Gothic
> towering of crystals in the trees
> Jock Neilson cutting a distant log. (105)

The rhythmic sounds lessen distances of both time and space; and the speech is vernacular, local and Australian. "Vernacular speech, then, along with the varying shades of southern light, sound and silence—all become luminous features of Murray's later work."[14]

The final section is a remarkable presentation of Australian topography followed by a sharing of different ideologies.

> *Black men and Rosenberg and I*
> *have beliefs in common*, I exclaimed
>
> and you were agreeing that Mao Tse-tung
> had somehow come to Dusinane. (107)

The impact of Australian landscape is such as to make the various points of view coexist. In this world, contradictions are not at war with one another; rather they are accommodated in a harmonic pattern of life. Finally the poet sums up:

> *Reality is somebody's*, you said
> with a new and wryly balanced smile.

We're country, and Western, I replied. (107)

Throughout the poem the use of the collective pronoun "we" makes the poem stand for the whole lot of people. It suggests the democratic humanitarian attitude of the poet. Peter Porter's comments on this last section are worth quoting: "At the end there is a characteristic Murray enrichment of definiton: baroque language, which the Australian bush has always cried out for but has customarily been denied, is confirmed by a witty social aphorism, a pun out of the media. This is the way Murray's Boeotians acknowledge the gods. . . . At last an Australian poet has stated the most important truth about his homeland." (45)

"The Mitchells" is one of those poems in which Murray has voiced some of his central beliefs about the Australian social ethos. The poem originally formed the epigraph to his book, *Lunch and Counter Lunch* wherein its title was "Dedication, Written Last: for the Vernacular Republic." The poem looks forward to the emergence of an egalitarian society in Australia. "The point of the poem is its depiction, from the outside, of an Australian Vernacular culture and its shared private understandings."[15]

The poem describes the two workers—the Mitchells who are taking their meals after digging a hole for an electricity pole. The poem functions in the present tense—present continuous tense in particular:

I am seeing this: two men are sitting on a pole
they have dug a hole for and will, after dinner, raise
I think for wires, water boils in a prune tin.
Bees hum their shift in unthinning mists of white

bursaria blossom, under the noon of wattles. (99)

The poet uses "dinner" for what the city dwellers call "lunch" suggesting his association and love for the country vernacular. He himself is not sure about the purpose behind the raising of the pole. Therefore, he says, "I think for wires." The whole setting is a country landscape wherein:

The men eat big meat sandwiches out of a styrofoam
box with a handle. One is overheard saying:
drought that year. Yes, like trying to farm the road. (99)

Penelope Nelson calls the first eight lines "exposition" because "they set the scene, introduce the characters and begin to quote their dialogue."[16]

But it may be recalled that in exposition the story does not move forward: it moves backward. And the poem simply exists in the present tense.

Of the pair, one has been rich
but never stopped wearing his oil-stained felt hat.
Nearly everything
they say is ritual. Sometimes the scene is an avenue. (99)

The conversation of the two workers is rather overheard by the poet, meaning thereby a poetic distance combined with a romance of remoteness which the poet has been able to maintain throughout the poem. Murray points out that he thinks of one of the Mitchells to be an Aboriginal. The poem in this sense epitomizes Murray's preoccupation with the notion of "convergence" of urban, rural and aboriginal cultures in Australia.

The world of Murray's poetry is one of masculine beauty and "The Mitchells" is a masculine poem in tone and texture. Alan Gould comments that there is "that idealized reticent masculinity in the men's speech, their peculiar modesty, and their peculiar vanity; their independence and the dour, slightly ridiculous deliberation in their thoughts and conversation."[17] The last line of the poem is remarkable in a number of ways. "Nearly everything they say is ritual"—here the word "ritual" has hardly any religious implication, since the work they are involved in is not a religious one. Yet if the root-meaning of the word "ritual" is followed which is "custom," we can say that their every gesture and speech is customary, typical of themselves. And the last line "sometimes the scene is an avenue" universalizes the basic idea behind the poem—the idea of a shared sense of belonging to a single community. "Casual meetings and observances, in Murray's sympathetic hands become the lasting ceremonies and cornerstones of the culture."[18] "The Mitchells" is one such cornerstone.

In "The Commonwealth of Manu" Murray refers to the four-fold caste system of the Hindus and how the same principle of distribution of social roles forms the basis of modern Australian culture and social set-up. Even in his country, society seems to resemble the Commonwealth of Manu:

Just for a moment
it seemed true of our country equally:
Brahmin, Kshatriya,
Vaishya, Shudra,

the four casts in our country, too, plus such as myself
and the genuine black men. (53)

The poet by dint of his profession belongs to an entirely different class. So do "the genuine black men." But the apple-cart of the balanced and harmonious social set-up as propounded by Manu has been upset in the post-industrial world by the dominance of "Vaishya" who symbolizes the big industrialists, supermarket business magnets and the multinationals. The world is ruled by money and the man who has it:

Vaishya, though, merchant, lowest of the twice-born,
consider his dominance:
the whole nation turning on him,
his the government, his the laws, his the profits,

his systems the System. (53)

The poet's effort to find a relevance of ancient Hindu culture and the socio-religious notions enshrined in it, to the modern world is really creditable because in doing so he seems to have successfully re-interpreted the social ethos of the post-industrial world: he discovers a link between the modern world and the ancient Hindu culture and its socio-religious categories. From this standpoint, Ganesha, the elephant-headed god whom the Vaishyas worship seems to acquire a new symbolic significance:

Consider the elephant
thick-skinned, intelligent, vast,
the beast of long affection, long revenge
capable of absorbing a whole pond.
Unable to jump. And very private at love.
Ganesha the God, provider of unearned goodluck,
has a lovable tusk, and a cobra for a belt.

His other face is failure,
Insanity, death.

Under the aspect, called Ganapati, he can
sometimes be appeased by a sacrifice of morals. (53-54)

In such a state of affairs, there is no place for the innocent maternal love of the cattle—since thick-skinned "elephant," symbolizing materialism and commercialization of life, reigns the world. The various epithets used by Murray for the elephant—"thick-skinned," "intelligent," "vast," "the beast of long affection, long revenge" and "very private at love"—on the one hand sum up quite naturally and realistically, the temperament of the wild animal the elephant usually is and on the other symbolize the big dons of the business world. It is worth noticing that "Although Ganapati, Ganesha and Gajanana are one and the same today, they were not identical in the ancient past."[19] Moreover, the lines—"His other face . . . of morals"—seem to refer to the fact that Ganesha as Ganapati Vinayaka in *Yajnavalkya-Smrti*, "is given the role of creating difficulties and abstractions if not properly propitiated." (21) Thus, in the Murrayesque Commonwealth of Manu, Ganesha, the money God can be "appeased by a sacrifice of morals."

Murray's most famous poem of rural Australia and Aboriginal culture is "The Buladelah-Taree Holiday Song Cycle," a long poem, in thirteen sections based in part on a translation by R.M. Berndt of "The Moon-Bone Song," a ritual poem of Arnhem Land Aborigines which as Murray claims "may well be the greatest poem ever composed in Australia." Murray's "Song Cycle" makes use of an Aboriginal mode and structure to celebrate "my own spirit country." The geographical location of this "spirit country" is a stretch of land on the north coast between the two towns of Buladelah and Taree, where the poet grew up and now lives as an adult and where many holiday vacationers go in summer to enjoy the beaches and the bush. For the poet these holiday outings of the vacationers to the country are a cyclic affirmation of ancestral values and a joyous communion in nature. "In his vision," says Paul Kane, "each new generation rediscovers the spiritual significance of commonplace things, as people come to possess the land imaginatively. Each section of the poem presents an aspect of this summer ritual." (290) About the composition of the poem the poet says: "As I thought about it, I realized it would be necessary to incorporate in it elements from all three main Australian cultures, Aboriginal, rural and urban. But I would arrange them in their order of distinctiveness, with the senior culture setting the tone and controlling the movement of the poem. What I was after was an enactment of a longed for fusion of all three cultures, a fusion which as yet perhaps, can only exist in art, or in blessed moments when power and ideology are absent."[20]

In this poem, the poet, keeping aside all the differences of opinions and ideologies, simply celebrates his vision of a ritualized happiness which only a well-knit and yet highly flexible community can enjoy. The very flexibility and broad-mindedness of the people of this community is responsible for the harmony that binds all together.

Section I of the "Song Cycle" may be regarded as the casual opening of the poem wherein the poet describes how the people are earnestly waiting for the return of those who have gone away to live in the cities. They are waiting for them for these visitors have deep associations with this ancestral region:

> The people are eating dinner in that country north of Legge's Lake;
> . . . they are thinking about relatives and inventory,
> they are talking about customers and visitors.
> In the country of memorial iron, on the creek-facing hills there,
> they are thinking about bean plants, and rings of tank water,
> of growing pumpkin by Christmas; . . .
> for this is the season when children return with their children
> to the place of Bingham's Ghost, of the old Timber Wharf, of the
> Big Flood That Time. (115-16)

This section at once brings to one's mind the mood of Chaucer's Pilgrims in the "Prologue" to *The Canterbury Tales.* The only difference is one of perspective; in the "Prologue" the poet joins the party of the pilgrims—the out-goers, a community-to-be initiated, Murray is already with the rural folk—the community of the initiated ones waiting for the vacationers. Otherwise, the mood in both the poems is the same one of celebration and jubilation. Moreover, like Chaucer's pilgrims who

> down to Canterbury they wend
> to seek the holy blissful martyr, quick
> to give his help to them when they were sick.

Murray's vacationers go out to the country and the bush when they are sick of the din of life in the city and also to gain some spiritual bliss and get revitalized emotionally and ethically.

This section also demonstrates that one of the characteristic features shared by all Aborigines is a general love for toponyms and certain legends evolved round those place-names, making them permanent myths in the life of the community . Thus, the poet refers to "Bingham's Ghost," "Old Timber Wharf" and "The Big Flood That Time." In his article "The Lore of High Places," Murray points out, "The Irish . . . had a word for it: *Dindshenchas*, the lore of high places. A scholar-poet of the old order lost face if he could not give a ready account of the traditions surrounding every notable hill and stream and fortress in the land."[21]

While Section 2 describes the Pacific Highway in peak holiday time as a great fiery but all-giving Rainbow Snake, Section 3 begins "the process of rediscovery of intimacy with landscape and familiar creaters. . . . Names of creatures begin to be capitalized . . . a sort of affectionate quasi-totemic empathy is suggested by this, a kind of a casual sacredness in well known things."[22] The poet says:

> It is good to come out after driving and walk on bare grass;
> walking out, looking all around, relearning that country.
> Looking out for snakes, and looking out for rabbits as well. (116)

The process of rediscovery is continued in Section 4 also where sheer observation is the first lesson in understanding between the human and the non-human:

> The birds saw us wandering along.
> Rosellas swept up crying out we think we think; they settled far ther along. (117)

In Section 5 the poet introduces the subject of ancestors and the way they are mentioned suggests their timelessness rather than sense of succession. These "Fathers and Great-Grandfathers," as the poet calls them, have become with the passage of time holy initiated beings to be worshipped by all and everybody. They are the chief custodians of the wisdom of the race which only they can impart to the generation since they have made the sacrifices; now it is their prerogative to preach. Our forefathers, unlike ourselves, knew that there cannot be any preaching without sacrifices. Hence, unlike our forefathers we are ignored by those whom we preach. To quote the poet:

> The Fathers and the Great-Grandfathers, they are out in the padocks all the time, . . .
> We tell them that clearing is complete, an outdated attitude, all over;
> we preach without a sacrifice, and are ignored;
> flowering bushes grow dull to our eyes. (117)

After Section 6 and 7 which are a mere celebration of the beauty and the meaning of sports of the rural folk and the vacationers, in Section 8, the poet mixes memory and perception so as to weave a poetic pattern wherein human work and human settlement are in perfect harmony. In this "blessed moment" of poetry and art, this harmony attains those ultra-dimensional heights where human work and human settlement interchange each other's roles:

Shapes of children were moving in the standing corn, in the child-labour district
coloured flashes of children, between the green and parching stalks, appearing and disappearing.
Some places, they are working, racking off each cob like a lever, tossing it on heaps;
Other places, they are children of child-age, there playing jungle.
(118)

Thus the corn-fields are the child labour districts and the "other places" are "the children of child-age" and they play "jungle." There is a perfect empathy between men, work and their surroundings producing a congenial environment for the celebration of life and nature.

Forests and State Forests, all down off the steeper country; mosquitoes are always living in there;
they float about like dust motes and sink down, at the places of the Stinging Tree. (119)

According to Pollnitz, "Section 8 is almost pure celebration." In this Section "the female and the male mosquitoes alternate as subjects, only displaced in a last subrodinate clause by human beings who, after being much acted upon, act themselves. They join in the dance."[23]

In Section 9, the poet refers to the workers and the ex-servicemen, the "warriors" who will have to bend the knee to find successors: "drinking from a tap/they watch boys who think hard work a test and boys who think it is not a test." Section 10 is again almost unalloyed celebration, of places and habits of the ibis, with peripheral human figures tentatively rediscovering "Things about themselves, and about the ibis."

Section 11 describes how the children learn about their ancestors through the toponyms and the ecology. The objects of nature teach them legends and true wisdom enshrined therein, about their forefathers:

The trees are split and rotton-elbowed; they the old-fashioned summer fruits
the annual bygones: china pear, quince, persimmon;
the fruit has the taste of former lives, of sawdust and parlour song, the tang of Manners. (120)

In Section 12 the poet evokes the season and the place by calling them by various toponyms. But it is in the final 13th Section that the poem reaches its climax. Unlike its great model "The Moon Bone Cycle," Murray's poem is "progressive in a loose sort of way" as a result of which the climax comes only in the final Section of the Cycle.

Here the poet elevates the land and the region and almost locates it to the heavens with "the Great Imagery of the Stars." "The region is *placed* in the universe and the whole experience of the Holiday, the walkabout quest, I mapped and sealed for the people who now have to go back to their other life."[24]

The "Song Cycle" is remarkable because of certain other features pertaining to popular culture. For example, almost every section has a reference to the family and the notion of the succession of life. The notion of an altruistic "we" and its continuity throughout the generations past and present is fundamental and central to Murray's poem. Whitmanesque in tone and form, the poem is a profound celebration of life "into the country of Communes." But the very profoundity of celebration is not a burden on anybody's soul. It is so light and lucid that the poet has not forgotten to make a reference to eating and drinking in almost every section of the poem. Only Section 13 is different and that too because the celebration enters the region of Logos and divine incantation.

Pollnitz regards "The Holiday Song Cycle" as "a classic Australian poem, both for the rich poise of its tone and the wealth of its felt detail." (195) According to him the details themselves seem to weave the pattern for the whole poem and this pattern seems to point towards an order or orders beyond the poem itself. Thus, the poem itself seems to exist in a poetic timelessness which, as Murray calls, is a "blessed moment."

But according to John Barnie, the poem "does not capture a moment of convergence between the three cultures, nor does it present a parallel to the cyclic experience of the Aboriginal poem,"[25] as Murray so fondly wished it to be. Barnie further elaborates his point and says that the poem "presents a moment in linear time, in a society governed by rapid change. The poem celebrates this moment for the one generation that can truly appreciate it, because its root experience was in the country." But the poem has been written by a white man. Whatever the poet's perspective of the country folks or the Communes may be, his perceptions are liable, unavoidably, to get coloured by his own white ancestry. But, Murray certainly has been able to place the poem in a universal context. It is his *tour-de-force* thus far as a writer and it demands—taking a phrase from Murray himself—a "non-judgemental looking into" from its readers and researchers.

In 1976, Murray won the C.J. Dennis Memorial Poetry Competition for this long poem. As Greame Kinross Smith remarks: "With its feeling for place and memory, its invitation to look again at Australia, language, landscape and people it is perhaps the best summation of Murray's work to date."[26]

The foregoing analysis of Murray's four poems seems to suggest that for Murray the poet, the notion of covergence of three cultures—Aboriginal, rural and urban—is one of the basic planks of what he terms as Vernacular Republic.

NOTES

1. Les Murray, "The Human-Hair Thread," *Persistence in Folly* (Sydney: Angus and Robertson, 1984), p. 29.
2. Paul Kane, "Notes," *Magillis Critical Survey of Poetry* (USA: Yale University), p. 289.
3. Ken Goodwin, "Mid-Century Directions," *A History of Australian Literature* (Melbourne: Macmillan, 1986), p. 215.
4. Thomas Shapcott, ed., *Australian Poetry Now* (Melbourne: Sun Books, 1970), p. 74. Qtd. David Headon "Naming the Landscape—Les Murray's Literary Language," *Westerly,* No. 1 (March 1983), p. 71.
5. Les Murray, *Quadrant* (April 1976). Qtd. Donald Horne in *Money Made Us* (Ringwood: Penguin, 1976; rpt. 1977), p. 229.
6. David Headon, p. 72.
7. Peter Porter, "Les Murray: An Appreciation," *The Journal of Commonwealth Literature*, XVII, 1 (1982), p. 46.
8. *Ibid.*
9. A. Bullock et al., *The Fontana Dictionary of Modern Thought* (London: Fontana Press, 1977; rpt. 1986), p. 666.
10. Craig McGregor, "Pop Goes the Culture: Academic and Other Prognostications," *Meanjin*, 1 (1980), p. 4.
11. Qtd. Craig McGregor, p. 5.
12. Peter Porter, p. 45.
13. Murray's poems are cited from his book *Vernacular Republic: Poems—1961-1983* (Sydney: Angus and Robertson, 1988).
14. David Headon, p. 73.
15. Les Murray, "Human-Hair Thread," p. 16.
16. Penelope Nelson, "The Mitchells," *Study Notes on the Poetry of Les*

A. Murray (Sydney: Methuen, 1978), p. 34.

17. Alan Gould, "*Vernacular Republic*: A Review," *Nation Review* (Nov. 26, 1976). Qtd. in Nelson, *Notes*, p. 35.
18. David Headon, p. 77.
19. M.K. Dhavalikar, "Origin of Ganesa," *Annals of the Bhandarkar Oriental Reasearch Institute*, LXXI (1990), p. 2. In *Yaganavalkya-Smrti*, Ganapati is both a trouble-maker and a trouble-shooter:

    Vinayakah Karmvighnasiddhyamarth viniyojitah
    Gananamadhipatye ch rudren Brahmana tatha.
    (For creating obstacles in the doing and fulfilment of Karma, Rudra and Brahmin made Vinayaka (Ganapati) the leader of the Ganas like Pushpadanta etc.).

    Taking a clue from this sloka, it may be suggested that Ganesha or Ganapati—the "lord of obstacles" and one who "can be appeased by a sacrifice of morals"—seems to represent the business magnets of today, who are the lords of obstacles—both creating them and then removing them. None but Ganapati could have been the God best suited to and worshipped by the Vaishyas—the merchant class of old, the supermarket dons of today.
20. Les Murray, "The Human-Hair Thread," p. 24
21. Les Murray, "The Lore of High Places," *The Peasant Mandarin* (St. Lucia: University of Queensland Press, 1978), p. 46.
22. Les Murray, "The Human-Hair Thread," p. 25.
23. Christopher Pollnitz, "The Bardic Pose: A Survey of Les A. Murray's Poetry—III," *Southerly*, II (June 1981), p. 192.
24. Les Murray, "The Human-Hair Thread," pp. 25-26.
25. John Barnie, "The Poetry of Les Murray," *Australian Literary Studies*, XII, 1 (May 1985), p. 31.
26. Graeme Kinross Smith, "'The Frequent Image of Farms'—A Profile of Les Murray," *Westerly*, III (Sept. 1980), p. 51.

Themes of Love and Death in the Poetry of Judith Wright and Sarojini Naidu

T. BHARATHI

Judith Wright and Sarojini Naidu are the best known and most widely read poets, whose reputation extends outside their native countries. There is something interesting and charming in their poetry, in the sense that, both these poets have reflected on certain universal themes like love, life and death.

When we think of the theme of poetry in general, we tend to think of traditional subjects like love, death, nature, religion, war. Thus Shakespeare becomes a love poet because of his sonnets, Wordsworth a nature poet and Emily Dickinson a poet of death. Love and death are common facts in every human being's life. So these two themes could not escape the attention of most of the creative writers. Although Dr. Johnson says in his *Preface to Shakespeare,* "Love is one of many passions" it is the chief and important passion in one's life. So it specially attracts the writers as well as the readers. Love, life and death, the essential factors in every person's life, are the focal points of this paper. The aim of the present study is to compare the poetry of Judith Wright and Sarojini Naidu on these specific aspects. Love and death, though very much attempted themes, every writer deals independently and with originality.

Judith Wright's poetry sings about the recreation of the Australian landscape—its people, its history and the way one influences the other, and an intense evocation of the spirit of place. Though Sarojini Naidu's early poetry showed Anglo-Saxon sentiments and settings, the later poems replaced the Anglo-Saxon sentiments and settings with the Indian. Their poetry ranges from exquisite vignetts of their native life—Judith Wright's "The Bullocky," "The Kite," "The Ancient Cycades" and Sarojini Naidu's "The Snake Charmers," "The Bangle Sellers" and "The Weavers" are a few examples of love as a divine feeling rather than mere passion.

There is sincerity and sensation in Judith Wright's love poetry.

Varalakshmi rightly points out: "Her frankness in expressing her passions can be clearly seen in poems included in *Woman to Man,* where her main theme is love." Her poems are "not the expressions of tempestuous desire, and for her the world of love is full of pain, parting and bereavement, privation and loss, which by the alchemy of her poetry she transforms into ecstasy." Sarojini Naidu's poetry too deals with sensuousness but there is no vulgar lust in it. As K.K. Sharma states, "The kind of love we find in Sarojini is actually inspired by the lofty Indian ideal of self-sacrifice. Her love poetry displays a variety of moods, irony, hope, despair, expectation, challenge and ecstasy. Both the facets of love—union and separation—have been comprehensively portrayed in her lyrics."

The other main aspect of their poetry is metaphysical; it aims at the spiritual mystery of human life in human relationships in Judith Wright and mystical love in Sarojini Naidu. In her love poetry Sarojini Naidu shows the multi-coloured love in joy, sorrow and mystic union.

To some people death is the leveller of all inequalities and to some others death transcends the human to unite with the Supreme Soul. So death is viewed differently by writers. Bhatnagar opines that death is created in the stereotyped images by the Indian English writers and thus shown as "a destroyer, a tyrant, a murderer, a servant of God, a guest, a lover or a beloved, a bridegroom or a redeemer spelling in turn either the mood of gloom, dissipation, futility, helpless acceptance or willing surrender." Death is an inevitable fact in everyone's life and poets sing of death. Hence the existence of number of elegies.

A.D. Hope shows how Judith Wright in her second book of poems *Woman to Man* differs from other poets in the treatment of the theme of love: "They have written much of love but not much of making love. And, as is natural for a woman, not only the act and the passion, but its outcome, the conception, the gestation, the birth and nurture of the child, are the subjects of the poet's meditation and the aspects of the world to which she gives an articulate voice."

Most of the love poetry by women poets deals with the opposite gender. However, they rarely express the "physical description or physical details of love making." This poetry challenged and offended many critics by its frank sensitive exploration of feminine emotions. At the outset these poems give the impression that they are portraying the physical love and it appears as though the world is centered round love-making but in actuality it is life-making.

Judith Wright has also written purely passionate, intensely personal and feminine love poems. A few examples are:

None but I shall know you
as none but I have known;
yet there is death and a maiden
who wait for you alone; . . .
so move in me my darling,
whose debt I cannot pay,
pain and the dark must claim you,
and passion and the day. ("Woman's Song")

And

This is no child with a child's face,
this has no name to name it by;
yet you and I have known it well.
This is our hunter and our chase,
the third who lay in our embrace, . . .
This is the strength that your arm knows,
the arc of flesh that is my breast,
the precise crystals of our eyes,
This is the blood's wild tree that grows
the intricate and folded rose. (*Woman to Man*)

A.D. Hope justifies these poems not as mere sensuous but the mystery of recreation. He says, "These opening poems are beautifully sexual but it is the sexuality of the whole mystery of reproduction, felt as one process and directed to one end."

Judith Wright's love poems are full of quiet passion and unspectacularly made. Though critics charge her that her love poetry deals with physical love, she uses that love at once for unity and creation. The unity of the people destroys loneliness, erases hatred and drives out fear. The feminine and motherly feeling is clearly seen in many of her poems.

The poem "A Song to Sing You" is addressed to a child who is yet to be born:

My heart made it,
my blood bore it,
my tongue spoke it,
the song of the child yet to be born.

In "Woman to Child," she dreams of the birth of child and talks to the child thus:

you who were darkness warmed my flesh
where out of darkness rose the seed.
Then all a world I made in me;
all the world you hear and see
hung upon my dreaming blood.

In the following stanza the poet moves from a mother to the universal Madonna when she identifies herself with Mother Earth:

I wither and you break from me;
yet though you dance in living light
I am the earth, I am the roof,
I am the stem that fed the fruit,
the link that joins you to the night.

Sarojini Naidu believes that love should completely surrender to the loved. In love there are only humility, lowliness and selfless service. It is a passion which is always ready to give for nothing in return. In her love poems we see and feel the traditional and age-long customs and adventures. She also emphasizes that no lover feels tired even if he was thousands of miles away; when his beloved calls him the lover finds it irresistible:

If you call me I will come
Swifter, O my Love,
Than a trembling forest deer
Or a panting Love,
Swifter than a snake that flies
To a charmer's thrall. . . .
If you call me I will come
Fearless what befall. ("If You Call Me")

"The Sins of Love" narrates love with concrete and sensible beauty. "Sarojini's love of physical sensations is unequivocally expressed in this poem":

To lure or to conquer your love
Its passionate love to appease,
To solace its hunger and ease
The wound of its sorrow or smart.

The best example for the poetry of self-surrender is:

Take my flesh to feed your dogs if you choose,
Water your golden-trees with my blood if you will,
Turn my heart into ashes, my dreams into dust
Am I not yours, O Love, to cherish or kill ("Love's Guerdon")

And

Why need you sad penance or pardon or prayer
For life's passion and folly and fears?
My soul be your loving atonement. O Love,
In the flame of immutable years! ("The Late-Song")

Sarojini Naidu's love poetry covers almost all aspects of Love. In "Village Song," the girl's feelings when coming back from the river Yamuna after meeting her lover are described. It becomes dark and she repents for the delay and prays Rama to guide her in the dark evening:

Full are my pitchers and far to carry,
Lone is the way and long, . . .
Unless Thou succour my footsteps and guide me,
Ram Re Ram! I shall die.

Without a mention of Radha's love, Sarojini Naidu's love poetry is incomplete. In the poem "Songs of Radha, the Quest" Radha searches for Krishna and asks wind, water and wood for him. This quest for the hiding lover is a redoing of the proto-quest that is mentioned in *Bhagavatam*, when on finding the gopies bloated with ego Krishna performs a vanishing trick. Then each of the gopies searches for Krishna and in the process questions every element of nature whether it has seen the divine lover. This quest has become the archetypal search in all devotional poetry, where the individual soul yearns for union with the Absolute:

My foolish love went seeking thee at dawn,
Crying—O wind where is Kanhaya gone? . . .
I am of thee, as thou of me, a part.
Look for me in the mirror of thy heart.

Another important poem on Love is "Pilgrimage of Love" which is divided into three parts and shows the pilgrimage of love towards the temple of sanctity. As Indu Goel explains, "The Temple" enshrines love, and the pilgrim has first to pass through "The Gate of Delight," and then has to proceed on "The Path of Tears" in order to attain "The Sanctuary."

Death is also one of the fundamental themes. Though many poets have written on death, Emily Dickinson is identified with the theme. For her, death leads to immortality: "The general symbol of Nature, for her, is Death, and her weapon against Death is the entire powerful dumbshow of the puritan theology led by Redemption and Immortality." Her poem "Chariot" may be quoted as an example:

Because I could not stop for death,
He kindly stopped for me;
The carriage held but just ourselves
And immortality. . . .
Since then 'tis centuries; but each
Feels shorter than the day
I first surmised the horses' heads
were toward eternity.

In Judith Wright's "Midnight," the central theme of the poem is death and rebirth. Death and birth are the eternal twins, and even in Christian theology resurrection follows death. It is a cyclic process through which every life has to pass, and this again can be traced back to the seasonal myth, which is effectively brought out by Shelley in his "Ode to West Wind": "If Winter comes can Spring be far behind?"

As a plant in winter dies
down into the germ, and lies
Leafless, tongueless, lost in earth
imaging its fierce rebirth; . . .
And with the whirling rays of the Sun
and shuttle stroke of living rain
weaves that image from its heart
and like a god is born again.

In the Freudian thinking there is the syndrome of Eros-Thanatos. Judith Wright in her songs "Love and Death" delineates this syndrome:

My eyes—rest upon you,
to me eyes turn,
as bee goes to honey,
as fire to fire will burn . . .
But so silent my heart falls

when you are away
I can hear the world breathing
Where he hides from our day. ("Our Love is So Natural")

Judith Wright employs a metaphysical conceit to describe the inseparableness of the lovers, in her poem *Eden.* Love, being an inner quality, seeks its partner in the inner being of the other. It is like two arcs being brought together into a circle. The two arcs are the lovers who find their fulfillment in the spiritual union of the circle called Love.

Where in predestined joy
and with a shock like death,
the two halves of my being
met to make one truth . . .
Yet where the circle was joined
the desperate chase began,
where love in love dissolved
sprang up the woman-man

Before exploring the theme and treatment of death in the poetry of Sarojini Naidu, one may ask whether she had any practical experience like Toru Dutt, who lost her brother and sister. She reveals her innocence on death in the poem "The Bird of Time." She invokes time to reveal to her,

The fragrant peace of the twilight's breath
And the mystic silence that men call death.

In "The Soul's Prayer," she exhorts:

Speak, Master, and reveal to me
Thine in most laws of life and death.

Sarojini Naidu does not merely live as a poet in the Cloud Cuckooland of romanticism but shows a keen social awareness in the poem "The Old Woman." She can empathise with the plight of the Old Woman who awaits her death. In this poem she portrays death as a form of sleep:

In hope of your succour, how often in vain,
So patient she sits at my gate,
In the face of the sun and the wind and the rain,

Holding converse with poverty, hunger and pain,
And the ultimate sleep that awaits.

"In Remembrance" is a poem written on the death of Violet Clarke, her friend. She looks at death as usurper:

Till Death usurped your vivid loveliness
In wanton envy of its radiant bloom?

Like Keats Sarojini Naidu laments over the loss of beauty when death comes. Death is a cruel villain that snatches away the lovely bride from her husband's caress. On the death of a young bride the poet's feelings are:

What longer need hath she of loveliness
Whom Death has parted from her Lord's caress? ("Dirge")

Though both the poets are sensuous in their love poetry and though both of them seem to be singing of love on the physical plane there is something more to it than the mere physical. Judith Wright's poems reflect on the continuity of creation and unity through love, love being a cementing force; Sarojini Naidu's love poetry sings of total devotion and surrender to the beloved. Love is no love when there is no sacrifice. Love is a quality that grows out to embrace the other. It is an eraser of the ego:

Love, I am yours to lie in your heart like a flower,
Or burn like a weed for your sake in the flame of hell.
("Devotion")

But these verses are criticized as "more rhetoric than poetry." In Sarojini Naidu's love poems the typical Indian ideal of self-sacrifice and complete surrender of body, heart and soul dominate. No personal feel of death is visible in her poetry.

Judith Wright strongly believes that it is only through love that threat, terror and fear can be overcome because love unites and creates. And though she is always conscious of the inevitability of death she continuously hopes for the renewal of birth.

This is to Mourn a Man: Judith Wright's "Interface I," "Interface II" and "Interface III"

MADHUMALATI ADHIKARI

The country grows
Into the image of the people
And the people grow
Into the likeness of the country
Till to the soul's geographer
Each becomes the symbol of the other. Max Dann

Creation and celebration of serious and genuine poetry can thrive only on authentic experiences and emotions. A poet's emotion, recollected in tranquillity interacts with the cultural, environmental and geographical factors of the past, present and future. All artistic creations explore twin questions: why and how? Undoubtedly, the artist creates to communicate and thus no one than the artist has a better notion of his obsessions, responsibilities, problems and ideas typical to him, often moulded by the circumstances and the milieu, to reflect and comment upon. The task of underlining and articulating the vital experiences of the poet, often very difficult, is carried out by the language and other artistic devices suitable for the purpose. These offer answers to the question of 'how.'

Australian poetry emerging from very different political, geographical and cultural syndrome cannot ignore the typical emotive objects of nature: the black snake, the grey lizard, the whale, the all circling sea, the sterile desert etc. These are the perceptual frameworks within which new conceptual ideas take shape. No Australian poet can either sing about the Nightingale, the light-winged Dryad of the trees, or the ethereal Skylark truthfully, except in a sense of nostalgia. The poet growing in the Australian soil has to dismantle the conventional images and satisfy his imaginative quest with the mundane whale. Poetic imagination has the power to weave the uncouth presence of the sea-animal meaningfully, into the beautiful fabric of poetry that lifts us from the immediate to the universal. "Great poetry does not teach us anything, it changes us for it is an existence and not a thought . . . a fire in the spirit, burning away what is mean and deepening what is shallow."[1] Judith Wright's "Interface I," "Interface II" and "Interface III," truly burn away what is mean, deepen what is shallow and compel us to ponder about the existential problems of man.

Judith Wright, the distinguished Australian practitioner of the poetic art, reluctant to plunge into the insubstantial and the fantastic romantic poetry, has turned to our world, riddled with problems of human relationships, pollution—physical and emotional, dehumanization that has led to a decline of our inner and outer worlds. In "Interface I," "II" and "III," it is not the whale's story that she narrates; it is the story of mankind through the ages. The concept of "Interface" used as a metaphor interprets human life through the analogy of a whale-story.

It is futile to attempt an analysis of these interlinked poems *sans* a recognition of Wright's motivating sensibilities. To Wright, poetry is "a human creative activity" and "not an academic subject of study."[2] She has the insight to perceive that man's materialistic pursuits dehumanizing in nature, the cause of innumerable miseries, can be decimated through poetry. Poetry can revitalize "imagination, vision and creation." (viii) The writer is a human voice, literature is a mirror, sometimes even a source of our values and our actions, our problems and our attempts to come to terms with them." (viii) Wright's genuine concern for man now a machine, over-fervent about "the new days reel/of punched instructions"[3] distanced from the nurturing natural environment and thus the self, motivates her to reflect upon the various confrontations in man's life—physical or emotional. She creates literature not because she is interested in its structure and language but because "it emerges from and reflects on our total situation as individuals and as societies." (viii) Wright is convinced that a writer must be "sensitive enough to what is happening in us and around us and to our humanity to ask important questions, and explore real alternatives." (viii) Her implication is obvious: a poet has an artistic-cum-social duty to perform. She is of the opinion that one should pay attention to "what they [the poets] say and imply, rather than the way in which they say it." But in Wright's poetry, we cannot ignore the 'way' of saying because "arts are the supreme form of communicative activity."[4] Good poetry inseparably combines form and content.

Wright's search of a meaningful existence for man motivates her constantly to examine and explore the crises of human lives. If she is shocked by the drab existence of women ("They"), she is also intensely alive to the limiting situations of human life that recurringly compel us to walk on tightropes ("Tightropes"), maintaining a precarious balance, "seeing no further than the pace or two ahead." (4) Hoping to escape from the critical issues, personal and universal, "sliding and slackening" into a half dream ("Half Dream," 9) tortured/by the worries of crime, death, confrontation, capture, betrayal, we may foolishly believe, "No one is dying, no body is being tortured/ this is the real world and perfectably safe" ("Dream," 10) but truth cannot be painted by these illusionary colours. Incapable of facing the challenges of life, we are destroying ourselves, committing suicides ("Interface I," "II," "III") and in no way are we wiser than the whales. The story of mutual oppression and exploitation is voiced, "but still the giants trample the sky" ("The Beanstalk, Meditated Later."[5]) A total breakdown of communication between man and nature has resulted in an overall deterioration of values and the cumulative effect is frustration and disillusionment. Like Wordsworth, Wright feels that the world is too much with us. Because of this malady, the call of the nurturing sea, "wait child, stay with me,"[6] is ignored by man. Caught in the trap of physical time identified with computers, we cry, "I would, I would, but time won't have it so." ("Interface I," 5) Though whales and men have evolved from the same element, that is, water, yet if the former had profitably remained close to her nourishing self, the latter, by abandoning her, has brought about nothing but disorganization and disorientation in their lives.

I.A. Richards in his essay "The Four Kinds of Meaning" posits that "articulated speech" (poetry is one of them) can be recorded from four points of view: "Sense, Feeling, Tone, Intention."[7] Thus to interpret a poem, we must not only take into cognizance these four points of view but also observe minutely how these act through symbols, imagery and metaphors. All words are symbols and in that sense the title "Interface" can be interpreted to denote the ideas and situations that meet face to face in the poem. "Interface" as a title is interesting and it presents a situation where man and the sea-mammal often stand face to face revealing the different inadequacies of their lives. These three interlinked poems, dominated by the sea and the dream imagery, composed in verse-paragraphs of different lengths and pattern with no regular rhyme scheme, express poetic imagination adequately through alliteration, assonance, the use of sibilants and alveolar sounds. The flow of the sea and the movement of the hectoring clock is well demonstrated with the aid of long-drawn vowel-sounds in words like "waves," "dreams" "meandering" or short and clipped utterances in "sit," "curtain," "stop," "hectoring" etc.

I

The poem "Interface I" begins with "Dreams: waves." (5) The poet by placing a colon in between illustrates, amplifies and equates the waves with the dreams. The similarity is further accentuated by establishing the fact that both tend to change and flow with the movement of the wind (raging in the mind or on the earth's surface) and have their limitations as neither can go beyond its shores. Dreams, manipulated by the waves of association and experience, dissolve on the shores of consciousness, and natural waves break into fragments, recede as they reach the shores. These two, constantly in a state of flux, make us recall William James' description of the human consciousness. Meandering waves and dreams evoke the memory of the meandering rivers that change their course arbitrarily. The word "meandering" with its syllabic divisions enacts the movement of twisting and turning. As the waves and the dreams roll either from the depth of the sea or from the abyss of the unconscious and the sub-conscious, their soft but critical messages reach us. The Freudian theory of dreams, its psychoanalytic explanation, illuminates the idea inherent in 'admonishing voices.' (5) Our "guilt" revealed through dreams, full of turmoil, foam and froth on the shores of consciousness. Man, too solid in substance, neither can go back to the depth of the sea, the source of the waves, nor plunge in the caves of the unconscious with a desire to reach the fountain of dreams. The muted rebuke apparently emerging from the sea, but really rooted in our conscience, constantly surfaces demanding our attention. Thus the poet perceives a similarity between the dreams and the waves. The comparison temporarily is halted and we are made to concentrate on human conditions. Man is ever restrained from enjoying the easeful bliss of dreams; the call of life, too persistent, awakens him; the disturbed sleep gives him the 'heavy head' that is also a reminder of the "guilt" that lies in the form of repression. He experiences a physical uneasiness; a feeling of suffocation, breathlessness and death overwhelms him. Man questions this physical and emotional discomfort and wishes to place the responsibility on some stranger. But ultimately, he realizes that it is his *own hand*, his *own choice* that has brought about the deplorable situation. The easy use of the belief that an uncomfortable positioning of limbs is the cause of bad dreams, highlights the poet's excellence in bringing the experience close to the reader. The mist of confusion disperses as realization percolates in. The image of the mist manifests the connectedness with the introductory imagery of dreams and waves, both misty inherently. The first verse-paragraph introduces the subject of "weight" on man's heart but leaves the question of "why" unanswered.

Through a systematic patterning of thought it is suggested in the last verse-paragraph of "Interface I."

The following short and clipped four lines describe our wakeful hours, incongenial to dreaming. Daily, "new days reel of punched instructions" is fed into us; we act like computers. To Wright, man's computerized existence, a form of oppression, is very disturbing. In "Typists in the Phoenix Building," she speaks of comptometers and calculators that "add up the years."[8] The outrage of the mechanical routine compels us to "sit up," "pull back the curtain." We are repeatedly subjected to the bullying tactics of the clock. Here, the poet focuses attention on the tyranny of the mechanical time. She insists, "I am not driven by clocks"[9] but is frustrated to see others enslaved by physical time. In "For M.R.," she formulates the several concerns of the poet: "Poems can chill, shock,/ stop you cold in your track,/ functional as an axe." (59) "Interface I" shocks us enough to recognize the deplorable state of affairs. Wright with her deep love of nature is distressed to see man alienated from his environment.

The concluding third verse-paragraph of "Interface I" describes man's final separation from his mother, the sea. Perched on his high-rise apartment ("far below") man can see the receding sea and hear its murmur. The final parting has a pleading prologue, "Wait child, stay with me." (5) Here, Wright weaves a myth and establishes clearly that the sea is the mother of man.[10] Scientifically also life has originated from the water element. Though man ignores the request yet it illustrates mother earth's deep affection for her children; it also illuminates the idea that she knows best. Wright's faith in nature as the eternal mother has never wavered. It is not that man consciously and succinctly repudiates the relationship but restrictions imposed by time compel him to respond regretfully: "I would, I would, but time won't have it so." (5) Time, a dominant image in Wright's poetry, is neither always demanding and tyrannical nor is she opposed to the changes of temporal time. In fact, like Eliot, she believes "time present and time past/are both present in time future"[11] and the present should look forward to the promising future. But in this poem, she indicates that the severing of bonds from sea, the mother, and accepting the bondages of time, does not necessarily usher in a new future. Most reluctantly man changes his allegiance because time, the autocratic commander, would not permit to continue this man-sea relationship. Human acquiescence to come to the shore of life with a sea of material needs lodged in their hearts and are compelled to abandon the natural surroundings. They crawl out of the 'bed' (of the sea that denotes peace), dress and rush to participate in the feverish activities of life. Though we humans are born from the sea yet we are "unfinned," demonstrating clearly that we do not entirely belong to the kingdom of sea-animals and thus physically and circumstantially we are doomed to live on land. Wright for the first time introduces the idea of the whales obliquely by stating we are finless. Since the new habitat is alien to us we "drag" ourselves and "crawl" (a behavioural pattern of water creatures). The story of evolution is cut short deliberately and decisively; the parting is made permanent as we put on a dress which itself is artificial. It is imperative to understand that our choice of land and material things, the root cause of divorce from our original habitat, is not imposed on us but is self-sought. Wright in the poem has hinted at man's evolution from the sea; it is the *aqua-vitae*. To appreciate Wright's artistry, we must take cognizance of the opposing images of the sea. One is the affectionate mother, ever protecting her offspring and the other is the betraying sea of greed lodged in our hearts. The poet, obviously unhappy with the prevailing conditions, regrets obliquely man's incompetent decision. Her tone can neither be ignored nor misunderstood.

II

"Interface I" begins with the scientific theory of evolution and "Interface II" reshapes the truth with a myth spun around man's acceptance and whale's rejection of land. Wright not only draws evocative images of the mother sea with the help of a myth created to formulate values and value the ways of life but also conveys her ideas through the story of the whales, another mammal. The last lines of "Interface I" make man's and whale's separation an unretrievable situation made perceptible by the selection of opposing places of habitation: land and sea.

"Interface II" begins with the description of a rugged beach strewn with round pebbles, the handiwork of the sea, the hunting ground of fishermen. The message is reiterated that though rising from the same source, man and fish, in essence brothers, are now eternal enemies: the predator and the prey. It is the repetition of the Cain-Abel story; the separation is final. It is a point to note that the sea-smooth rocks look like whales. This sea-change (cf. *Tempest*) can be brought about only by the sea. Gradually, the idea of dead whales is introduced. The happy illusion of rocks being whale-like is shattered when a small dead whale is discovered. Death enters the scene, never very far from life, not through our imagination but through reality. Ironically, the small dead whale is now lifeless like a rock. The inter-penetration of life (whale) into death (rock) and death into life suggests the closeness of these two absolute truths. In fact, life and death are placed face to face, interface like waves and dreams, whale and man. The idea of interface is repeated to highlight opposition and confrontation.

The dead whale described as the "decaying monument" is dead, thus decaying and its size is a reminder of a monument. The use of the word monument is very interesting. In *Twelfth Night* Shakespeare uses 'monument' in an inanimate, inarticulate sense. A monument on man is erected after death. But the whale is a monument to itself. Elizabeth Bishop, the American poet, uses the concept in "The Monument." It is made of wood and has the "eroded air." (45) Here too, Wright's monument is decaying. The similarity between Wright's and Bishop's ideas though coincidental is thought-provoking. The whale now a monument not organic or dynamic but static with its "sunk eye-sockets" is a confirmation of death. Wright's power of observation is established as she compares the "sunk eye-socket" with the "dry" withered temples of old people, dear to us. Once again life and death is juxtaposed focusing our attention on "other things," the tragedies of life: the "sad" victims of time, loved but not saved from the decaying effect of old age. The exposition of the inner meaning through the inter-penetration of situations, true to humans and animals, exhibits Wright's capacity to move from the "closed" to more "open" connotations of human life.

If in "Interface I," Wright hints at the opposing ways of life opted by men and whales, in "Interface II," she offers a mythical explanation of this antipodal choice. The analogy is introduced not to enhance merely the superficial beauty of the poem but to insist that the history of man and the whale if not identical is similar. Off-springs of the same mother, they meet their end in a similar way through the suicidal act. The third verse paragraph narrates the myth of the whales. As a precursor of man (man being much junior in the history of evolution), lured by the materialistic existence, the sea-mammals had experienced land-life but since they had found it uncongenial and inadequate they had abandoned it and returned back to the "mothering upholding element," (6) the sea. The return was easy. An unprotected life away from the mother is difficult and cannot be borne by all. Wright is surely critical of a situation that motivates one to remain in a restraining cocoon. The whale's easy return to its mother and the "half-sleep" condition is not recommended by the poet. Sleep implies inaction, ignorance. The question that is being raised obliquely is, "Does life mean sleeping?" The answer to this question though not directly available, is suggested by the next lines that doubts the decisions of the whales. If they were satisfied with their decision, where was the need to commit suicide on land? They had rejected land and materialism and strengthened their bonds with nature, then, why this wilful tragic end? Wright weaves a peculiar but a common happening of the Australian life into the poem: the beaching of the whales on the sea-shore that ultimately results in their death. "They choose their suicides." (6) The poet, exploring their psychology, imagines the conflicts, the depression and offers an explanation of the suicidal act. The "wind battered" beaches, reminiscent of the harsh experiences of life, make them recall their failure to accept the challenges of life and hence, a psychic turmoil, a "guilty" feeling that finally drives them to self-slaughter. Wright not only weaves a new myth around the intriguing behaviour of the whales but also incorporates the Freudian theory of suicide that automatically sanctions a ruminative power to the whales that can feel guilt.

The last seven lines of the poem reiterate the similarity between man and the whale: their source of birth is same and so is their final "choosing" of death. The whales had rejected the land mass but man had chosen land, abandoned the faithful mother sea "to face a challenge." Ironically, they too end their lives by drowning themselves in the sea; they too suffer from the guilt of rejecting their mother; they too had failed to face the challenges of life. Thus, they go back to mother sea profound and forgiving, to surrender. The "cross-traffic" of whales reaching the shores to die and man turning to the sea to drown himself, points at two different types of guilts in man and whale though the outcome is no different. In Wright's poetry, earth with its land, vegetation, sea represents creation. Man in search of materialistically satisfying life alienated from the forces of creation is ultimately disillusioned and destroyed. "Interface II" closes with a sense of ambivalence: it is neither helpful to reject the challenges of evolution (like the whale) nor wise to severe completely the relationship with nature (like man). It is interesting to recall that by incorporating words like "cross-traffic," "guilt," "failure," "challenges," the bane of human lives, Wright moves from the specific to the universal, from the distant past to the present.

III

"Interface III," the longest of the trio, continues to delineate the theme of death and suicide introduced in "Interface II," the result of "guilt" rising from "unaccepted challenges." Wright rightly feels that it is a type of madness, a mental disorder (as diagnosed by medical science) that propels man and whales towards self-annihilation. The complex working of the mind at the root of a suicidal act, often referred by the psychoanalysts, is woven into the poem. With a single-mindedness, the whale selects a spot and its movement comparable to ships controlled by insane captains, meets nothing but inevitable destruction. Massive as the liners, with the "worm" of "death wish" lodged in its brain, it elects death as no amount of manoeuvring can return it to its life saving source (cf. Plath, "Mussel Hunter at Rock Harbor," "died recluse or suicide," 98) The inner treachery leads to self-destruction, a characteristic symptom of the disease, the poet believes, is seated firmly in the brain. The poet describes a natural phenomenon, offers a scientific explanation and hints at similar human behaviour. Wright is disturbed by the ideas of treachery and betrayal ("Dream") and their destructive role in man's life.

Death always ushers in a radical change in the object and the environment. If in "Interface II" death had solidified the small whale into a rock and bared the bones of the eye-socket, now, in the next stage putrefication sets in (see Plath "Suicide off the Egg Rock"). The coastal air is "tainted," polluted with the stench of dead flesh and the overwhelmingly disgusting smell spreads all around like "corruption." The use of the word "corruption" is very subtle and suggestive. It is a reminder of the modern corrupted life that encircles us; it can be felt but not touched; it being all pervading cannot be buried because of its gigantic size and its intrinsic insubstantiality. The shift from the concrete to the abstract enlarges the range of the meaning. The lifeless body of the whale transforms the scenario of the beach. The foul smell of the rotting flesh makes its removal imperative. But no sand is deep enough to bury the large carcass. Thus, it has to be further mutilated, cut into pieces (man's destructive role is stressed) and bulldozed away by men wearing masks to protect themselves from all types of infections that come with decay, death and decomposition. The ugly drama of death, often enacted on the Australian beaches, described meticulously, is staged to do away with the offensive "smell of death." But can the smell of death be obliterated when there exists "pursuit," "capture," "hunger," "torture," "betrayal" (see "Dream," 10). This is a question that is ironically and indirectly raised by the poet. Another question closely associated with the previous one is implied: can man remain untouched by death? Though the poet apparently seems to be concerned about the stench of rotten flesh and death of the whale yet the real issues before her are: the corruptions, senseless destruction in man's world and the eternal presence of death in every sphere of human life. This implicit idea surfaces from the wreckage of decaying flesh.

Artistic texts use analogy to frame universal ideas. Repeated comparisons underline the affinity between man and the whale. According to the poet, both, despite being mammals, have equally, fatally, failed in their lives. Misinterpreted dimensions of existence have directed them towards self-annihilation. The poet requests for clinical analysis to detect the "virus" of self-destruction. Interestingly enough Sylvia Plath also finds similar tendencies in human beings when she remarks in "Crossing the Water": "The spirit of blackness is in us, it is in the fishes."[12] Poets are often considered as prophets and seers and surprisingly enough, a very recent discovery has succeeded in isolating a unique gene in the brain of man that instigates suicides. Wright has been prophetic unconsciously. The poet on the one hand wishes to dissect and analyze the problem of whales, and on the other she is convinced that they are "past cure." The whale-road[13] has been finally abandoned by them. In the last verse paragraph the poet concretizes her disquiet regarding the suicidal path that people, countries, nations, galaxies have been pursuing through the ages, destroying each other. This mutually ruining confrontation, Wright also alludes to in "Birds": "But I am torn and beleaguered by my own people . . . /and my heart is the house where they gather and fight/for dominion."[14] Implied in this fact of collective destruction is a question, "Why this confrontation and self-annihilation?" The answer is offered in "Dream." Greed, jealousy, hunger, betrayal, frustration are the inevitable causes of self-destruction. The wars, Wright believes, the glaring examples of suicidal acts in which nations participate, are perpetrated for "the narrow self-interested nationalism and inflated power dreams." Her conviction is articulated in many of her poems. "Interface III" closes with the lines, "But this is to mourn a whale" that deliberately attempts to dislodge our attention from the many-hued human problems but in the process, the reader is convinced that "Interface I," "Interface II" and "Interface III" are composed to mourn a man.

Devoid of classical references, the cluster of poems, simple, lucid, euphonic, exquisitely balanced in sound and sense, formulates an unconventional rhyming pattern. Despite the ease of conversation, the inter-connected poems have satisfying depth for the discerning reader as Wright quite often through the description of typical Australian life, arrives at profound truths (see "Dream," "Eastermoon and Owl," "Australia 1979," "Bullocky," "The Beanstalk Meditated Later," "Brother and Sisters," "Birds," "Legend"). Basically, man's suicide-wish (also probably a whale's) is triggered off by his failure to walk on tightropes (Wright concretizes failure in "Brother and Sisters"). It is a self-sought destructive, inevitable situation that man opts for when he decides to abandon mother nature. Wright, a great modern poet, has incorporated the authentic feelings, character and the cultural syndrome of her land. She has successfully projected the decadence that is undermining the very presence of man on this earth. By framing the dangers of life, Wright provokes us to search for a new meaningful balance between desire and responsibility, materialism and love of environment that would enable us to conquer failure, avoid suicide and live the life of the blacksmith's boy in "Legend":

> The blacksmith's boy hung the rainbow on his shoulder
> instead of his broken gun.
> Lizards ran out to see,
> snakes made way for him,
> And the rainbow shone as brightly as the sun. (Wollman, 75)

NOTES

1. W.B. Yeats, *Uncollected Prose*, ed. J.P. Frayne (London: Macmillan, 1970), p. 187.
2. Judith Wright, *Because I was Invited* (Melbourne: OUP, 1975), p. vii.
3. Judith Wright, *Fourth Quarter* (London: Angus and Robertson, 1976), p. 5. All quotations from this text.
4. I.A. Richards, *The Principles of Literary Criticism* (New York: Routledge and Kegan Paul, 1929), p. 17.
5. Harry Heseltine, ed., *The Penguin Book of Australian Verse* (Ringwood: Penguin, 1972), p. 289.
6. Compare the call of the Merman in Matthew Arnold's "The Forsaken Merman."
7. I.A. Richards, "The Four Kinds of Meaning," in David Lodge, ed., *20th Century Literary Criticism*, *A Reader* (London: Longman, 1989), p. 116.
8. Heseltine, p. 288.
9. *The Writers*, Archival Film Series: Australian Council, 1987; Judith Wright interviewed on film by James Murdoch.
10. Compare Matthew Arnold's view of the sea in "To Marguerite": "The unplumb'd, salt, estranging sea."
11. T.S. Eliot, *Four Quartets* (Delhi: OUP, 1962), p. 13.
12. Sylvia Plath, *Collected Poems* (New York: Harper Perennial, 1992), p. 190.
13. In Anglo-Saxon poetry, the sea is termed as the "whale-road."
14. Maurice Wollman and John Spencer, ed., *Modern Poems for the Commonwealth* (London: George G. Harrap, 1966), p. 22.

Judith Wright and the White Goddess: A View of "Fourth Quarter" and "Easter Moon and Owl"

URBASHI BARAT

The lunatic, the lover and the poet
Are of imagination all compact.

William Shakespeare

It is my nature
as woman and poet
to give birth
over and over
always to birth
a daughter, a son, a poem;
  to nurture the seed/the young
  to start again and again
  to see in the old, the new—
                the whole
  again and again

Alma Villanueva

Femininity and creativity have been closely linked together in the ancient myths of all cultures, in the great figures of the Earth Mother and the Mother-Goddess in their creating and nurturing, in Natura, Lilith, Demeter, Astarte, Shakti, Saraswati, Athena, the Muses, the Graces, all feminine, are the traditional inspirers of poetry. As Laura Riding points out, however, though "femaleness" has long been "associated with divinity . . . from an instinctive sense of appropriateness,"[1] the act of creation itself is traditionally masculine.[2] Riding goes on to relate an ancient Japanese myth about the origin of poetry, which she believes is 'a caricature' of the male viewpoint, in which the goddess Iza-nami-no-mikoto, on seeing the god Iza-nami-no-mikoto for the first time, exclaims out loud in praise of his beauty. This greatly displeases the god who believes that as a male he should have been the first to speak. So they encircle the great central column again, and now when they meet it is the god who praises the beauty of the goddess, and his words become the origin of poetry.[3] Robert Graves, Riding's companion for many years, used this story in his famous work on the nature of poetry, *The White Goddess*, to suggest that the Sun-god had taken over poetry from the Moon-goddess, pretending he had originated it: "With that, poetry becomes academic and decays until the Muse chooses to reassert her power, in what are called Romantic Revivals."[4] Thus it is that Judith Wright's Eve, calling the story of Creation in Genesis a masculine invention to cover up for man's insecurities, asserts her conviction that femininity is the root of life and creativity:

I could never believe
that old rib-story you told.
You, to come first? It was Night, Water,
Earth, Love, I.
You, Adam, son of the Sun—
you thought his maleness chose
you out of the unshaped clay
(his huge masculine beard, his dictator-hand
giving you strength. But I—
I *was* the clay.

Eve Scolds

The first two poems in Wright's 1976 collection, *Fourth Quarter*,[5] the title poem and "Easter Moon and Owl," grow out of this perception of creativity, using as their basis the most traditional symbol of femininity and creation in Western culture: the moon. The moon is the White Goddess of Graves's book, the Queen and huntress chaste and fair whose potency images that of the Virgin Mary on the one hand and the Earth Mother on the other. Lunar imagery sees woman as fertile, waving and waning in her monthly cycle, and part of the generative processes of the earth. Above all, she is the symbol of the instincts and the passion, the ruler of the night and the unconscious, and the source and the inspirer of poetry.

"Fourth Quarter" is a wry acknowledgement of the poet's advancing years, but it is also a defiant assertion of the undying human spirit of creativity that will not be stilled even though the body itself might fail.

You bitter sign,
last lemon-quarter grin,

tell me to throw it in?
I won't resign.

The woman, like the moon is in the last quarter of her life; both will soon be obliterated in the darkness of the night, but while the moon will always 'make a comeback' (l. 8), the woman can never do so. That is why the waning crescent moon is a 'bitter sign,' a sour (hence 'lemon-quarter') reminder of human decay and mortality, its Chesire-Cat 'grin' suggestive of the pain and the derision behind the moon's knowledge of the woman's fate and the woman's own recognition of her frailty; 'grin' is repeated in the last stanza, this time as a verb—'Grin in the sky' (l. 18)—linking the end of the poem to its beginning and emphasizing the feminine defiance of mortality:

Grin in the sky,
I'm taker still and giver:
there's your reply.

The circular movement of the poem, reinforced by the repetition of 'grin' (and the fact that it is used in the two major grammatical categories in English, the noun phrase and the verb phrase), re-enacts the moon's varying phases in order to contrast the journeys of the goddess and the woman and to underline the feminine challenge to mortality.

Poets usually envisage a smiling moon, or invoke the full moon: even Sylvia Plath, for whom the White Goddess is most often Hecate, not Artemis-Selene, a 'bony mother' ("Moonrise") without the maternal instinct, and symbolic of sterility and death ("Childless Woman," "The Moon and the Yew Tree"), speaks of the lunar 'O-mouth' ("The Rivals") and 'O-gape' ("The Moon and the Yew Tree").[6] Wright's moon here, the narrow crescent that approximates a smile without mirth, has little kindliness, and seems to mock human aspirations. But she is not Plath's grieving, despairing 'great light borrowe[r],' 'beautiful, but annihilating' ("The Rival"); though she may grin she remains for Wright the symbol of the cycle of earthly and human regeneration, quickening poetry through her magic.

The woman and the poet, then, refuses to accept the grinning moon's suggestion to 'throw it in'; even the rhyme-scheme of the first stanza (abba), in which Wright states her defiance, sets it apart from the ones that follow (which go abab), so that the challenge in the last line of the stanza, 'I won't resign'—note the word-play (*resign/re-sign*)—becomes more important than the moon's knowing grin. For she knows that the power of poetry, as precious and as eternal as gold, still lives in her, though she herself

> won't be back again
> or not this way.
> But still there's gold to win
> from the mullock's clay.

The strikingly appropriate (especially for an Australian, whose country is noted for its gold mines) mining image suggests the nature of the poetic quest and recalls the golden artifact, the traditional symbol for the immortality of art, especially as contrasted with mortal human beings. Towards the end of her life Wright's poetic powers may perhaps be thought to have exhausted themselves, as a gold mine may be over-worked in course of time, but even if what is left of her is but 'mullock,' mining refuse, her 'clay'—the earth, the human body, and human frailty—can still yield gold.

The 'gold' surfaces when the poet is touched by another kind of gold, the gold of the moon's 'last-light tongue,' (l. 16) which, like the Pentecostal tongues of flame that had moved Christ's disciples to spread His word in languages they had never known before, continues to arouse and inspire those who can feel it. The moon's tongue is at once a reawakening of poetic sensitivity and responsiveness and its expression in poetry; and its touch makes the poet 'shiver' (l. 17) with the thrill of inspiration and creativity (cf. Milton's 'Lycidas'). 'Shiver' is also a reminder of the coldness of the moon, a coldness which, ironically, brings poetry to life: a work of art is shaped by the warmth of the emotions and the chill of impersonality working together.

The woman may seem 'old, terribly old/to the scornful young' (ll. 13-14)—is there an echo of Yeats's 'Sailing to Byzantium' and 'The Tower' here?—and the ambiguous syntax makes this equally applicable to the moon, and strengthens the kinship between the two; but in the end the poet will triumph even in the face of mortality:

> I'm taker still and giver:
> there's your reply.

—the brevity of the assertion conveying its finality. Poetry, then, is a continuing process, as cyclical, as it were, as the moon's seasonal path: the poet takes from the environment and from the moon, and returns something as infinitely valuable: her emotions and her poetry. Above all, the poet, like poetry itself, can never die; as woman and as poet, she will continue to create as long as the moon continues to move and she to 'shiver' in response.

This theme is further elaborated in the second poem from *Fourth Quarter*, 'Easter Moon and Owl,' in which the relationship between femininity and poetic creativity is clearly and explicitly examined through its exploration of the mythical kinship between the White Goddess and the woman-poet. Wright exploits in this poem the ancient identification of Easter with Eostre, the old English goddess whose festival was celebrated at the spring equinox and whose name is closely linked to those of the Roman Aurora and the Greek Eos, Dawn, the sister of Selene—indeed, the word *Easter* is derived from the same root as *east*, from where dawn, the new day, begins—and with the Semitic fertility deity Astarte, who from classical times had become part of the Artemis-Diana cults.

Easter's commemoration of Christ's Resurrection is a promise of regeneration; hence its special association with dawn, and in the northern hemisphere with spring. In the southern hemisphere, however, Easter coincides with autumn. Thus it is a most appropriate symbol for an Australian woman-poet in the autumn of her life, who, just as appropriately, invokes Eostre-Astarte-Selene as her Muse here. The goddess keeps faith with the world in her seasonal cycle, ushering in spring and a new day in the north at Easter but autumn in the south, where it also marks the northward departure of the sun for a long half-year.

> Keeping your old appointment,
> spring's northern dawn,
> you bring in autumn here.
> The god's long done for in this hemisphere;
> your full-tide flood of light
> won't set him rising.

The colloquial discourse (here in the first stanza, for example, there is 'keeping your old appointment' and 'long done for') and the closeness of the verse to the rhythms of speech emphasize the intimacy between woman and goddess; the dismissive note in 'done for,' moreover, with its hidden implication of being defeated, ruined, helps to reinforce the impression's superiority over Helios—as Eve had remarked contemptuously in 'Eve Scolds,' 'Sungods are parvenue.' This is further established by the alliterative finality and the chiming half-rhymes and assonance of the last comment in the stanza, 'your full-tide flood of light/won't set him rising.' That is, even all the creative powers of the moon, all her life-giving energy, which raise the tides in earthly and human bodies, minds and emotions, cannot bring back the sun to the southern hemisphere for the next few months; even the poet, no matter how powerful her poetry and her instinct for life, can call back the years of her physical prime, when the sun shone brightly overhead.

The moon, then, is no mere reflector of the sun's light but is a source of illumination herself (contrast Plath's "The Rivals" here): a deliberate reversal of the commonly held notions of the roles of sun and moon and male and female, and an affirmation of the moon's, and the feminine, power of creativity. This is underlined by the careful omission of the expected prefix 'sun' before 'god,' accomplishing thereby the inclusion of whatever is merely male/masculine within the ambit of her scathing dismissal. 'Flood of light' is, accordingly, no casual application of a neo-Platonic expression; it underlines the goddess's control over the waters of the earth and in the human body and psyche, which create new life, physically and in the arts. *Fiat lux!* was, after all, God's first creative decision, and it was from water that life first emerged on earth. Both light and streaming water are, moreover, common, perhaps even archetypal, images of poetry: see, for instance, Coleridge's "Kubla Khan."

Though Easter has different associations in the two hemispheres (vernal in the northern and autumnal in the southern), its universal message, its call to life, regeneration and creativity, is conveyed to both worlds by the owl, whose nocturnal habits, solitary state and proverbial wisdom make it for the poet the White Goddess's familiar (this is of course a traditional idea; compare, for example, Coleridge's "Christabel"), her 'ancient messenger' and 'servant,' whom the poet must 'greet,' for he is the link between the two hemispheres, the three worlds, and the woman-poet and the 'Ruler of women/and singler-out of poets' (ll. 9-10), whose call echoes the universal poetic belief in the close relationship between femininity, divine, chthnonian and human, and the poetic muse. The masculine qualities that the owl represents make him—and men—clearly subordinate, if not subservient, to the moon's feminine powers. Interestingly, where the moon-Muse herself is addressed familiarly and informally, the style becomes formal and 'rhetorical' when the poet refers to the owl.

This contrast between the feminine and the masculine is now worked out further. Men feel no sense of identification with the moon, nor realize what she is. For them the moon is an object to be studied scientifically, from the outside and from a distance: 'Men spy you out with eyes.' (l. 12) Note the pejorative connotations of 'spy' and 'eyes': the moon's influence is a subjective one, and must be felt instinctively and emotionally, and not merely observed externally and clinically. The masculine desire for possession, conquest and exploitation is a violation of the goddess's privacy and selfhood, and a denial of the instinctual, the inner life, characteristic of femininity:

> Their red brand's on your flank
> and they plan colonies.

The image of branding (Australia is a cattle-rearing country), reinforced by the use of the word 'flank,' the 'red' mark of possession, and the characteristic masculine term 'flank' even when used for a deity, suggest, too, their aggressiveness, their lack of sensitivity, and the barrenness of their endeavours. That is why women will never

> make it
> into those well-controlled
> and solar-heated settlements.

Woman's domain is much vaster, the entire natural world that cannot be confined within the kind of lunar 'colonies' men plan out. The artificiality of '*solar*-heated' contrasts with the natural 'chill' of the night and moonlight; the sun, it may be noted again, is male in every culture. Women are the 'true citizens' (l. 15) of the moon; men are only selfish, greedy and insensitive colonizers.

Yet women continue to bear man's burden, and to arouse his emotions and poetic instincts: the phrase 'drag his tides' (l. 19) points to the heavy slowness and reluctance of the male life-instinct. Even so, it cannot help responding to the lunar fascination as it does to the feminine one. For man's blood is after all salt like the sea, and like the sea must move to the pull of the moon as it does to the spell of femininity; witchcraft is instinctive to women, the protegees of Hecate, and binds men to the feminine principle in a primeval bonding.

Addressing the Easter moon not just as Selene but as 'Domina' (Wright's feminine form of the more traditional Latin *dominus* 'lord, master'), on the lines of the old Latin prayers *Dominae dirige nos* 'Lord, direct us' and *Dominus illuminatio mea* 'the Lord is my light,' the poet makes

> the prayer of age. In my last quarter
> let me be hag, but poet.

An old woman may well be a 'hag'—note the word-play, for 'hag' refers to both an ugly old woman and a witch—but as a poet she can continue to enchant through her creative magic. Her poetry may have lost the lyricism of youth, but the White Goddess as Hecate will accept the poetic offering of the 'hag,' for it is genuine poetry, whether it seems a spell or a curse.

When, therefore, 'they' mock her poetic Muse (the indefiniteness of 'they' is important, for 'they' is opposed to the 'us' of the third stanza, and as such refers to not just men and to all those male/masculine-minded people who cannot and do not respond to the moon-Muse), they will not be able to affect or to deny the moon's influence.

> Muse, if they mock you,
> you may yet grin last.

The waning moon's crescent is not a sign of her departure or defeat but a 'grin' of triumph and unshakeable superiority, the word linking it to "Fourth Quarter" and emphasizing the moon's ineffable pre-eminence. In its echo of the proverbial 'last laugh,' Wright's somewhat tentative 'you may yet grin last' becomes a certainty. Man's obtuseness, his need for conquest, are a threat to the living world and to poetry, which is born under lunar influence—'Man's signs are ominous'—but the moon's grin is a promise, a reassurance, of the continuity of the human spirit and the vitality of the poetic instinct even in old age and the reminders of human mortality.

NOTES

1. Laura (Riding) Jackson, *The Word "Woman" and Other Related Writings,* ed. Elizabeth Friedmann and Alan J. Clark (NY: Persea Books, 1993), pp. 29-30.
2. *Ibid.,* pp. 34-35.
3. *Ibid.,* pp. 41-42.
4. Quoted by Friedmann and Clark, *Ibid.,* p. 3.
5. Judith Wright, *Fourth Quarter* (London: Angus and Robertson, 1976).
6. Sylvia Plath, *The Collected Poems*, ed. Ted Hughes (NY: Harper, 1992).

The Changing Face of Australian Literature: Some Multi-Cultural Novels

RON SHAPIRO

In this paper I wish to discuss three books which make an interesting perspective on an Indo-Australian connection in Australian literature. I shall then proceed to discuss some important implications stemming from this examination.

The first book I wish to discuss is called *The Time of the Peacock*, first published as a single volume in Australia by Angus and Robertson in 1965, though previously published in separate episodes in the Bulletin during the 1950s. The 1950s in Australia was a period remembered for, among other things, the infamous White Australia immigration policy—in fact it had been in place since Federation in 1901. But in the years immediately after second world war, the Australian government of the day made a concerted effort to increase Australia's population through a programme of massive immigration under the slogan "populate or perish." The thinking of the period advocated a populous Australia with a view to deterring what at the time was popularly called "the yellow peril" to Australia's north—referring to the people of east Asia in, but by further extension to all the Asian hordes which were imagined to be waiting to pounce and take over Australia, not to forget "the red peril" which of course was Communism. In this period the government established an "assisted passage" scheme designed to bring to Australia as many Anglo-Celtic people from Great Britain and western Europe as possible. My own parents's family of six people (masquerading as Anglo-Celtic) reached Australia from Britain in 1949 for about £20 per family member under this scheme.

The Time of the Peacock by Mena Abdullah (assisted by Ray Mathew) consists of a series of interlinking stories concerning an Indian family which settled in the Australian countryside of New South Wales in early part of this century. Although a beautifully written book conveying a sparkling sense of Indian family life in the back blocks out among Australian sheep-yards and paddocks and gum-trees, *The Time of the Peacock* was never considered part of the major Australian literary canon—presumably because the Australian canon tended to favour bushmen and Aussie battlers of solid Anglo-Celtic stock. Similarly few other non-British nationalities ever appeared in white Australian writing; the Australian aborigine, to name just one obvious instance, was seldom ever mentioned.

Much of the charm of the interconnected stories in *The Time of the Peacock* has to do with the family's almost total isolation from Australians, both individual Australians and Australian society, apart from a neighbour Mr. Angus on an adjoining property and an occasional itinerant Irishman like Paddy-the-Drunk, or Hussein Khan who was a young Indian born in Australia and so was regarded by the family as a sophisticated man of the world. The family itself consists of a Muslim father and an ex-Brahmin but now converted mother together with their three children, Rashida, Nimmi and Lal. The stories are narrated through the eyes of Nimmi, the young daughter, and the sense of a child's understanding of life is wonderfully maintained through the verisimilitude of a child's point of view. An excerpt from the opening page will convey something of the narrative skill:

> When I was little everything was wonderful; the world was our farm and we were all loved. Rashida and Lal and I, Father and our mother Ama: we loved one another and everything turned to good.
>
> I remember in Autumn, how we burned the great baskets of leaves by the Gwydir and watched the fires burning in the river while Ama told us stories of Krishna the Flute-player and his moving mountains. And when the fires had gone down and the stories were alive in our heads we threw cobs of corn into the fires and cooked them. one for each of us—Rashida and Lal and I, Father and our mother.
>
> Winter I remember, when the frost bit and stung and the wind pulled our hair. At night by the fire in the warmth of the house, we could hear the dingoes howling.
>
> Then it was spring and the good year was born again. The sticks of the jasmine vine covered themselves with flowers.
>
> One spring I remember was the time of the peacock when I learnt the word secret and began to grow up. After that spring everything somehow was different, was older. I was not little any more, and the baby came.
>
> I had just learnt to count. I thought I could count anything. I counted fingers and toes, the steps and the windows, even the hills.

> But this day in spring the hills were wrong.
>
> There should have been five. I knew that there should have been five. I counted them over and over—ek, do, tin, panch—but it was no good. There was one too many, a strange hill, a left-over.

The humour here attests to the author's technique, her literary, as well as philosophical, approach to the world. Not only from a technical standpoint is the charmingly childish point of view rigorously held in this passage and in this story, but "reality" (whatever the word means) is seen to be intricately connected with language and with thought and with numeracy: if Nimmi cannot count accurately to five she always finds she ends up with a hill left over. This kind of demonstration of the way language skills construct what we call "objectivity" anticipates (in a very painless form) the claims of a more agglutinous kind of post-Sassurean contemporary critical discourse in many Western universities. Although perhaps more relevant to India are certain lines in the Prasna Upanishad which a long time ago conveyed the idea that the physical world is primarily created out of consciousness.

The family in this story lives in Australia but constructs an Indian world to live in on their property Simla Farm set out in the Australian countryside. The mother surrounds the house with a garden of Indian jasmine and Kashmiri roses. Ama leaves saucers of milk out at night for the snakes though her disbelieving Muslim husband secretly tips the milk away so as not to attract them to the house. The whole family is often seen at work in the kitchen preparing the spices for what seems an endless array of curries and other Indian foods in a land where ingredients are plentiful. The children's life consists in gently growing up, listening to the stories of India told by their parents and their Uncle Seyed, and in exploring the Australian fauna which surrounds their farm. For example, there is an episode concerning a "rusilla" which is in fact their mispronunciation of rosella, a colourful Australian parrot which (humorously for the reader) the four-year-old Lal believes he sees transmogrified into a variety of variant forms ranging from a stone replica of a bird in a nearby small town to a kitchen tea-kettle whose shrill whistle as the water boils reminds him of the "rusilla" he had wanted to keep as a pet. On a different occasion there are the kites they fly in a paddock near the house and which always seem to attract the attention of an eagle which the four-year-old Lal decides to call the Maharajah, king of the sky; the children are seen creating their own private ritual to appease the Maharajah just before they release their kites into the sky. This is a family which lives for itself and in a distinctive Indian way, and which because of remoteness has to make its own society. A rare occasion in the novel when the children come into contact with Australian children almost turns to disaster and ends in a brawl when the Australian children make fun of these Indians in their unusual clothes and decide to provoke them by calling them Nigger.

Interestingly, though, there are more memorable instances of intractable racism or xenophobia displayed on the Indian (that is, the Muslim) side than the Australian side. For instance, when a young friend of the family, Australian-born Hussein Khan, wants to marry an Australian girl his father is prepared to disown him. The girl is after all a Christian and an eater of pig and cannot properly continue the Khan family line. An equally inflexible position is taken by another friend of the family Uncle Seyed who argues that Islam is the only right religion and Muslims have a duty to their own, no matter what else. But the mother's Brahminical attitude is more tolerant; she argues that mistakes will always be made, this is human nature, but that all paths will eventually be seen as the right path. In fact her prediction comes true in that Hussein's father softens his attitude once his son's first child is born.

Set and written in an Australian period of fairly trenchant xenophobia, a period when migrants were supposed not just to integrate into Australian society but to assimilate—meaning to become like white Australians—*The Time of the Peacock* displays the wide cultural gap existing between Australians and Asian immigrants. This is a family which has little to do with Australians, knows very little about them, yet seems to regard them with a kind of awe, as the mysterious Other. The novel establishes a wonderful series of Indian vignettes among the crows and kookaburras of the Australian bush. Finally, however, these examples of Australian fauna remain secondary to the primary image of the Indian peacock which lives in their garden on Simla Farm, representing an identity which has little to do with the southern landscape they occupy.

The next novel I wish to examine is Adib Khan's *Seasonal Adjustments* published by Allen and Unwin in 1994 and set in a period ranging from the 1970s to the near present day. The main protagonist Iqbal Chaudhary, the son of a wealthy Bangladesh ex-zamindar family, migrates to Australia in the 1970s in a period of Australian history when a new Labour government was replacing the infamous White Australia policy with a new and more flexible immigration programme which was to slowly lead to a more multi-cultural Australian society.

In *Seasonal Adjustments* Iqbal, a Bangladeshi, decides to make a return visit to the family in Bangladesh after having spent some sixteen years in Australia, having married, and recently separated from, a white Australian girl from a conservative Catholic family background. He takes with him to Bangladesh his young daughter who is the product of this Australian marriage. The novel is concerned with inability he discovers in himself to fit back into the social patterns of Bangladesh society he had grown up in.

But the novel is more than this; it is first of all a juxtaposition of two societies and two cultures, Bangladeshi and Australian, and it employs a story which highlights the strengths and shortcomings on both, and on all, sides. Human beings in this novel, no matter their nationality or ethnic background, are seen locked into familial and cultural or ideological positions which prevent them from stepping outside of a narrow range of the fixed assumptions and attitudes they grew up with. Cultures and nations, the book shows, are not homogenous entities; there is no such thing as a typical Australian or a typical Bangladeshi or typical Indian; in fact the range of differences which exist within any single culture or society may be as great as the more obvious differences which separate the various societies and nations from each other. When Iqbal returns to the ancestral Bangladesh home after years in Australia he realizes that he has changed more than he knew; for instance, he has acquired the detached viewpoint of an observer and realizes that from the fairly strict Muslim viewpoint of his family his own remarks are regarded as little more than blasphemous facetiousness. He finds that here he is not supposed to speak his mind openly but is expected to observe a range of formalities and proprieties. He feels that his parents are once again resuming their old role of planning his life and deciding what is good for him, and more particularly for Nadine his Australian-born daughter for whom they are already thinking of suitable marriage prospects. Even in talking with people in social situations he finds he must take care not to give offence by, for instance, talking too much to another man's wife even if she is a relative. Whenever he tries to desist or to challenge family attitudes he is told, "You cannot change our ways. It is a custom our family has always followed." (47)

But equally strict and narrow are the attitudes of his wife's Australian family who have never really been able to accept him because of his difference. Particularly obnoxious is Keith, his father-in-law who stands for conservative white Australian values, but whose attitude is riddled with hypocrisies.

> What makes me unacceptable to Keith, even dangerous, is not my colour or my background. It is my refusal to uphold what he considers to be the immutable virtues of every decent Australian—a blind devotion to the monarchy, an active support for the policies of the RSL, a life-long membership of the Liberal Party and an undying belief that Australia should continue to draw

> all its spiritual and cultural sustenence from Europe, even in the distant future.
>
> Although Keith's dislike for the Japanese is particularly intense, at least he compliments them inadvertently, by identifying the people by their specific nationality. As for the rest of us, from the dark, unknown regions of the north, we are lumped together as Asians, recognizable by our absence of Christian principles which outweighs any discernible differences in ethnic characteristics. We are devious, unscrupulous, greedy and godless. Our unstated philosophy—copulate and populate. We are a bunch of untrustworthy ratbags extending our sinister shadows to blight the country he claims to be God's gift to Christians. (87)

Iqbal is equally irritated by the Australian suburban ways of life in which he sees a terrible inertia and triviality:

> Suburban life is comfortable and conducive to cerebral inertia. I live in a lovely area, shaded with wattle and gum trees, quiet and unpretentious. Like a good Australian I have been seduced by the common dream of a brick-veneer house on a quarter of an acre of land. The neighbours, unlike the free-roaming koalas, are polite and amiable from a distance. There's Tom and Bev. Nick and Penny. Gavin's been recently divorced. Brian and Jane. The others are a composite of hands and faces. We wave to each other and occasionally discuss the state of the backyard vegie . . . er, vegetable . . . patch, the fickleness of Ballarat's weather, and the rising cost of living when we meet at the local supermarket or the petrol station. On weekends we reinforce the cult of community uniformity by starting up our lawnmowers within minutes of each other. On Sundays you can almost swear the neighbourhood is a discordant industrial forest alive with the noise of manicuring machines. (122)

But Adib Khan does more than simply juxtapose two cultures to criticize. For in the course of the story his character Iqbal becomes aware of his own hypocrisy and double standards. While he is aghast at the disease and the plight of the poor he encounters in Bangladesh, and while he rails against the unmerited privileges of his own family zamindar background, he slowly uncovers a similar patrician arrogance within himself and in his own attitudes. So, for instance, when he learns that the family's wealth has been seriously depleted he realizes that he is affronted because of the loss of dignity this implies for the Chaudharies and for himself. Or while priding himself on his Western liberalism he is surprised at his own shock when his sister hints at a lesbian relationship she is involved in. Iqbal's return to Bangladesh forces him to confront his own unacknowledged prejudices.

Increasingly the subject of the novel transcends cultural difference and personal idiosyncrasy to consider human life and the human condition. Is the relative openness and freedom of Western society really any better than the set conventions in Bangladesh? Has British colonialism in this part of the world done much more than entrench inherent class snobberies and illusions of superiority? Was the war of West Pakistan against the eastern wing which led to the formation of Bangladesh anything more than conniving politics at its worst; and is *all* war really an officially sanctioned opportunity for the pursuit of male blood-lust despite the high-sounding official or religious rhetoric which usually accompanies it? Is it ever possible for humans to shed their restrictive cultural baggage, to free themselves of their solipsistic blinkers to behave fairly and impartially; or will familial, dynastic, cultural, or nationalistic imperatives always take pride of place in human thought and behaviour, always make any possibility of accepting, or even tolerating, the Other a wholly academic ideal?

To set oneself apart from the normal constraints is always likely to involve personal pain and suffering, a condition which seems in particular to be the migrant's lot. But for Iqbal it is finally not just the *only* option available, but the *best* option available since marginalization, deracination, loneliness, forces a reappraisal of everything one has always understood, assumed or taken for granted:

> A Bangali can be just as indifferent, mean, egotistical, loving, creative, heroic, generous, humane, cruel and greedy as an Australian. It makes you appreciate the homogenous blueprint of human life. It is this impossible mixture which binds humanity, and I am a part of it. No better or worse than anyone, but an equal. An equal because I know I am a composite of all those contradictory characteristics which are far stronger than any racial or religious differences. And that is worth celebrating. Difficult for you [to] understand, isn't it? You who allow yourselves to be blinded by your pride in a singularly blinkered tradition which fertilizes the grounds of bigotry. (143)

This note of defiance might be taken as a positive summation of Iqbal's marginalized position. In spite of the pain of separateness the modern individual, the author seems to say, must learn to stand alone and to cope.

The third novel is called *The Ganges and its Tributaries* by Christopher Cyrill and published in 1993. This is a first, and one suspects, largely autobiographical novel about an Indian family and its many immigrant relatives set in Melbourne in the recent 1980s. The story is again told in the first-person by the family's Australian-born adolescent son and concerns this period of his adolescence, his sporting interests, his girl friends, and the family's adaptation to a new country.

Although many of the same issues as in the books already discussed reappear in *The Ganges and its Tributaries* (problems of inter-racial relationships, of abandoning certain past ways of thinking, etc.) these difficulties are by no means as acute. In fact for the main Australian-born son Christopher they are not problems at all. This young man is good at sports, is involved in Australian football as much as cricket and hockey, barracks for Dennis Lillee and Australia in the India-Australia test series, suffers from no major instances of racial discrimination, seems to make friends easily with both sexes and has a regular non-Indian girlfriend.

And this easy untroubled relationship with Australian society also extends to Christopher's numerous uncles who are themselves relatively young and as yet unmarried men. The behaviour of the uncles is often on the point of scandalous, pinching girls' bottoms, calling out to passing young blonde women in the street, driving cars that blare the first few bars of Happy Birthday on the horn. Perhaps some of this behaviour is characteristically Indian at least in certain quarters; but it fits very easily into what is usually called Australian male ocker behaviour, the kind of larrikin male behaviour (which, I should add, has been subject to considerable attack in Australia in recent times, especially from women and feminists and the media more generally).

The Ganges and its Tributaries is, at least to some extent, reflecting a more contemporary Australia compared with the previous two novels I have discussed. Although at several points in the novel Christopher affirms his Indianness he is in obvious ways far more comfortable with Australian than with Indian customs. He feels embarrassed by the clothes and the sing-song English accents of his relatives when they arrive from India, he appears perfectly at ease with his sexual responses and there is no hint of coyness in his attitude, he at times even feels like a foreigner in the midst of his many visiting relatives. Even his parents seem to adapt quite easily. His father often goes shooting with some Aussie work mates, while his mother turns down an opportunity to return to India for a holiday, arguing that there is nothing much to see apart from crowds and hardship. While Christopher's grandparents still believe in the need to retain racial distinctiveness, his father argues that soon the world will consist of a single human gene pool and it is futile to swim against the tide. This is a novel which looks forward with a reasonable degree of equanimity to the time when the Ganges and its tributaries, and other corresponding ethnic river systems throughout the world, will all end up in the same sea.

Throughout the course of the last century Australian literature has undergone some momentous changes, but none so great as the changes that have resulted from a growing multi-culturalism over just the last decade. The last few years have also seen the appearance of a new kind of literary criticism—not just so-called "post-colonial" criticism which is already well-entrenched but also a less ideologically motivated kind of criticism seeking a more open, less academic, reappraisal of ideas pertaining to Australian identity in the late 1980s and the 1990s. Some important recent titles in this regard are *Images of Australia* (1992) edited by Whitlock and Carter, *Life in the Margins* (1992) by Jan Pettman, and *Striking Chords I* (1992) edited by Gunew and Longley, books which argue not only the existence of a contemporary multi-cultural literature, but that the emergence of this new literature has caused us to re-read the older literature in order to reassess past assumptions concerning a homogeneous Australian identity.

In my discussion of these three novels with a common "Indian" theme I have tried to signal the changes that have occurred within Australian society in the attitude towards non-European immigrants, but equally the changing attitudes of immigrants themselves towards Australia and Australians. In *The Time of the Peacock* non-Europeans lived in Australia in the late 1940s and the 1950s either as individuals or in a small isolated family group with minimal contact with Australian society; this family resides in Australia to escape the harsh regimen of life at home; they are in Australia for the immediate opportunities but see few longer term prospects for themselves in a foreign country. In *Seasonal Adjustments* we find ourselves in the 1970s and a period which saw the start of a more open Australian immigration policy. Iqbal Khan is married to, but separated from, a white Australian girl; his trip back to India is marked by uncertainties on all sides. In *The Ganges and its Tributaries* we have caught up to the present day; there is a general loosening of old attitudes, a new flexibility, a less rigid sense of racial distinctiveness and separateness on the part of both immigrants and Australians, and in the Australia-born narrator all the signs of what some postcolonial commentators like to call a new "hybridized" cultural identity.

It is of course perilous to read too much of a sociological nature into works of fiction which of their very nature are dialogic and polyphonic rather than simple single assertions or affirmations about the state of the world; nevertheless the first-person narrators in these books do to some (differing) degrees serve as authenticating and legitimizing witnesses to the kinds of changes I have discussed. And although it is equally perilous to build an argument on such a broad theme around a small sample of texts, I should explain that I selected these particular titles because of their Indo-Australian interest. However I might equally have taken examples of immigrant Chinese writing, or immigrant Malaysian writing, or immigrant Greek writing, or immigrant Italian writing, etc. It has recently been calculated that in the post-war period Australia has received greater numbers of immigrants than any other country except Israel. More than six million of Australia's current nineteen million population are the direct producers of post-war immigration consisting of over hundred different nationalities. And today more than 40% of all current immigrants are non-European. No longer can Australian identity be defined in terms of a past tradition of the bush and bushman, or by the successive more recent tradition of beach and suburb dwellers. Since the Australian bicentennial enactment in 1989 Australians have become more aware than ever before of the complexities surrounding the issue of identity. Australian aborigines argued that Australia was not "discovered" by Captain Cook or by anyone else since they were living there all the time. Feminists have argued that the writing of Australian history has always been written by males and about males, a point Kate Grenville made in her interesting recent novel *Joan Makes History*.

We are now in 1995. It was as recently as 1969 that Australian conservative immigration Minister, Billy Snedden commented: "We must have a single culture. If immigration implied multi-cultural acitivities within Australian society, then it was not the type Australia wanted. I am quite determined we should have a monoculture with everyone living in the same way, understanding each other and sharing the same aspirations. We don't want pluralism."

In the space of less than thirty years much has changed. Whatever Australian identity now means it means a plurality rather than any single set of defining characteristics. The polyphonic voices of Aborigines, migrants, feminists, homosexuals, environmentalists, academics, business representatives, the media, and so on, have eclipsed older more comfortably stereotypical monocultural definitions. Australian identity in the forthcoming new century is going to mean many identities and is going to require a new kind of sophistication and broad tolerance which thousands of years of global history have so far seldom managed to achieve.

Nations without States: The Search for Home in H.H. Richardson's *Fortunes of Richard Mahony* and Yasmine Gooneratne's *A Change of Skies*

JOHN MCLAREN

Nations are defined by their boundaries, but these boundaries join as well as separate. Continental nations contend with each other to establish geographical boundaries that will separate them from other states, only to find that acts of contention over their borders join them in common histories. Island nations are separated in space and linked in commerce and intercourse by the oceans that surround them. Australia, a nation inhabiting a continent that is also an island, shares some characteristics of both. As an island, it has provided a destination for migrants who have made it a meeting place for diverse cultures. As a nation state it has tended to turn its back on its surrounding oceans and, ignoring its actual commerce with neighbouring and source cultures, erect boundaries of difference.

Each succeeding wave of migrants has given a distinct shape to this difference. The Aboriginal inhabitants, for whom the sea was more a barrier than a link, turned their differences inward, producing distinct cultures shaped according to different geographic zones, but sharing a common apprehension of the relation of people to land. Lines of trade and song joined the cultures in a comprehensive network and, later, links developed in the north with Melanesia, the Malaccas and even China. This pattern was dislocated by the irruption of the British settlers who from the end of the eighteenth century incorporated the Continent in the British Empire, and thus joined it irrevocably with the processes by which industrial capital unified the globe. These processes in turn produced the waves of British and other migrants who came to dig gold and stayed to develop agriculture, deep mining and manufacturing; of refugees from religious and political oppression in nineteenth century Europe, and of later refugees from the chaos of northern and central Europe and the poverty of the Mediterranean after the Second World War; and, most recently, of refugees and others from the nations that have succeeded the old empires in Asia.

Two novels, published at either end of the twentieth century, deal with the cultural conflicts of the first and the latest waves of migration. The conflicts the characters endure are surprisingly alike, but their responses are dramatically different. The migrants in Henry Handel Richardson's trilogy, *The Fortunes of Richard Mahony* (London: Heinemann, 1917) and Yasmine Gooneratne's *A Change of Skies* (Sydney: Pan Macmillan, 1991) are displaced from island colonies, Ireland and Sri Lanka respectively, yet carry with them a wider sense of nationality based on imperial loyalties to an idealized island of Great Britain. While this sense preserves their self-esteem in their new country, it also alienates them from the emergent continental nation of Australia where they find themselves. In Richardson's trilogy, this alienation is resolved in tragedy. Mahony, finding no state to give him a home on this earth, retreats into the solitude of madness. Gooneratne's novel, by contrast, is a comedy in which the displaced characters, by entering into the lives of others, produce a community which is located within their new state but represents a nation that goes beyond any boundaries. This conception of a nation as a place of meeting rather than an enclosure provides the basis for a new conception of nationhood appropriate to contemporary interdependent internationalism.

The image that connects the two novels is the change of skies. It is introduced first in Richardson's novel when Mahony, taking a night-time stroll after his wife's musical card-party, encounters his neighbour Tangye, "The owner of a small chemist's shop on the Flat, [who] contrived to give offence in sundry ways." Irreligious and an occasional drunkard, Tangye lives with a woman not generally believed to be his lawful wife, and is suspected of engaging in nefarious practices to compensate for a lack of respectable trade. To Mahony, whose moment of contentment he interrupts, he represents every kind of defeat the colony threatens. The Latin phrase he quotes, which recurs as a leitmotiv through the trilogy, makes the defeat imminent by establishing the kinship between the young doctor on the eve of prosperity and the older man gripped by failure. "*Coelum, non animum, mutant, qui trans mare currunt.*" Those who race across the seas change their skies, not their souls. Tangye has failed because he has been unable to abandon his past, his true self, and adapt to the ways of the new country, the "hardest and cruellest country ever created," where only greed prospers, and every finer feeling, every scrap of wit or learning or intellect is destroyed. Mahony reluctantly recognizes Tangye's revulsion as his own, and sees in his own unwillingness to bend, in his moral distancing of himself from his neighbours, a portent of similar defeat. (305-8)

The central irony of the trilogy is that Mahony's changing fortunes, both his prosperity and his eventual plunge to disaster, come as a consequence of his two acts of surrender to the spirit of greed that he condemns in the others around him. His success in capitalizing on inside knowledge of the stock market enables him to abandon useful work as a doctor and indulge in what he considers the higher pursuits of the mind. His attempt to use the wealth of colonial gold to support a civilized life in Ireland and England is thwarted by the narrowness of those who have never changed skies and who, consequently, have no souls to alter. For a time, back in Australia, his wealth enables him to live the fashionable life in which his intellectual pursuits are sheltered by his wife's colonial generosity, but neither intellect nor hospitality connects him more than temporarily to those around him. When, after another impetuous chancing of his fortunes, his wealth disappears, the symbols of his intellect become symptoms of his decay. Only his wife's practicality, and the rewards of her earlier generosity, provide any succour during his last, terrible years.

In encompassing Mahony's destruction, the land fulfills the prophecy made in the novel's opening pages, where the shifting sands of the Ballarat goldfields bury alive the miner whose "passion for the gold . . . an almost sensuous craving to touch and possess" had led him recklessly to omit "to slab the walls of the drive." It had held him, like all the other miners, "ensorcelled" as it waited, "stretched like some primeval monster in the sun, her breasts freely bared, [watching] with a malignant eye, the efforts made by these puny mortals to tear their lips away." ((3, 11) Mahony deceives himself by believing that he has been able to tear his lips away and escape the greed and cruelty that has ensnared his fellows. He is in fact wilfully oblivious to the source and condition of his ease, blinded by his allegiance to an ideal British civilization that never was.

The character of Richard Mahony is the antithesis of both the real and the ideal Australia, distinguished from the former by Mahony's nobility of aspiration and from the latter by his perception of the sky as alien. Appropriately, I first heard of the novel of his fortunes while sitting in assembly at Ballarat High School. The headmaster, a figure of stature in every sense at a time when school teachers were still scholars, attempted in his weekly talks to introduce his students to a world wider than our immediate surroundings. As I recall, he presented Mahony as a noble figure from Ballarat's past, and the novel as a work in which we should take pride. Yet the Ballarat of the novel is vastly different from the one we knew. Both had a similar population, some 50,000, but whereas the citizens of Mahony's time were consumed by a restless fever for gold, those of ours were filled with a pride bordering on complacency that the dreams of the prosperity Mahony saw at its dawn had now been fulfilled. The city was a small version of the cities of northern England, with its own bank, its own insurance and trustee companies, its own newspaper, brewery, engineering works and biscuit factory. The time of gold was still recalled by the mullock heaps dotted about and by the fifty odd pubs that slaked the thirsts of the golden city. But these were outweighed by the respectability of over thirty churches, by the Alfred Hall and the Britannia Theatre, by the statues of Burns and Shakespeare passed by the trams in Stuart Street as they carried their cargoes of students to the city's own public schools at its western end: the end which Mahony had toiled so assiduously to reach from the mudflats and goldfields of the east. The victory of the mind over vulgar materialism for which Mahony had striven was symbolized by the annual South Street musical contests, the botanic gardens with their conservatory and statuary, and the regular visits of travelling orchestras and solo performers. Certainly, the School of Mines which had in the 1860s challenged Melbourne's university with its own degrees and professors was now merely a technical college, and the independent university which has since risen from it retains neither geographic, nominal nor formal connection with its origins. But, back in 1947, the continuing supremacy of the mind was demonstrated by the visit to the Alfred Hall of the Body Neil String Orchestra, which competed with the sound of stream locomotives shunting in the neighbouring railway yards to demonstrate that Britain still ruled the Empire of Civilization.

The Fortunes of Richard Mahony provides us with only two alternatives to materialism. One, represented by Richard, seeks a civilized ideal that goes beyond any single nation but ignores the economic reality that supports it. Its image, the sea, where alone Richard feels at peace, symbolizes constant change, but is also the vital medium without which the wealth of the Australian soil could not have been transported to world markets, and so provided the basis of Mahony's fortunes. The other, represented by Mary Mahony, is the land itself, or rather the society that has grown on it. Mary's practical strength and courage, and her emotional sympathy with others, enable her to control circumstance, but this control is equivalent to the greed of the miners plundering the earth, or the way entrepreneurs like her brother, John Turner, bend their energies into remaking the old world in the new country. While this new world has an energy and a largeness, a freedom from the customary bonds of the old world, it is, unlike Richard, tied to its immediate time and blind to the violence it does to the land that support it. It is thus unable to comprehend the vengeance the land harbours for its despoilers, which is realized in the novel in the devastation of the depression that destroys the burgeoning confidence of Ballarat and

Melbourne, and in the insolvency and descent into madness that destroys Mahony.

The Britain that provided both the model and the enemy for the citizens of goldrush Ballarat remained dominant in Australian consciousness at least until the middle of this century. The erosion of the bases of this dominance had, however, begun much earlier, not only internationally but within Australia. It was eventually destroyed not only by a developing national confidence and by new waves of immigration, but also by economic changes which integrated Australian industry first nationally and then globally. First casualties were such pockets of provincial independence as Ballarat, most of whose local enterprises were swallowed up by national companies during the first post-war decade. With this independence went the confidence that had sustained their attempts to maintain British culture. Just as Mahony left first Ballarat and then Melbourne, only to find that his native Britain now rejected him, so first Ballarat and now Melbourne have come adrift, lacking a past that can sustain an economic function or a cultural role in a global future. The economic and cultural energies of Australia have shifted from the interior and the provinces to the cities of the coastal north-east. These are the energies that encompass the characters in Yasmine Gooneratne's novel as they change the skies of Sri Lanka for those of Australia.

Nevertheless, despite the distance in time, Bharat and Navaranjini Mangala-Davasinha bring to Australia the same cultural attachments that Mahony brought a century earlier. Unlike Mahony, however, their sense of cultural superiority is in conflict with their anticipation of a racial hostility that will prevent them taking their proper place in the new country.

Both the hostility and the superiority provide themes for the extracts from the diaries of Edward Mangala-Davasinha, the grandfather of Bharat who, in the last century, ran away from his family home in Matara, Ceylon, and enlisted himself with a cargo of Sinhalese labourers being recruited to work in the Queensland canefields. Through the novel these diaries provide a counterpoint to the lives of Bharat and Navaranjini in their new land. Edward, described in the volume of his journals edited by his grandson as an 'Asian Grandee,' is thoroughly Anglicized, and, like Richard Mahony, finds the Australian settlers uncouth. He gives this difference some historical context by contrasting the styles of the British governors of Ceylon and those of the Australian colonies. The former had been from the landed gentry and had viewed their dominion "much as they would have viewed a well-stocked game reserve." As "Landowners who value their stock" they had recognized the wisdom of taking into their service "men who know the terrain and are already resident on the land." (162) By contrast, the Australian governors were plain men like Macquarie who, although they may have "worked tirelessly for the improvement of the rough settlement he had been sent out to rule," was "misunderstood and even disliked by the settlers." (163) These men lacked the aristocratic qualities needed to transplant the hierarchical British order which, Edward believes, the settlers would have welcomed.

Yet while Edward resembles Mahony in his belief in British order, he shows an adaptability more characteristic of Mahony's wife Mary. Just as he is prepared to disguise himself as a labourer to travel to Australia, so in the new country he is willing to accept any employment available. He thus discovers the bleak side of the Australian dream, going as a stockman to Badagini in Western Australia, a "dry and desolate place" where he discovers that a score or more of his countrymen had died of heat and thirst only a generation earlier. Although the Sinhalese had taken pains to learn of the country from the Aborigines before embarking on their attempt at settlement, they suffered the consequences of attempting to impose a foreign culture of husbandry on an alien land. This episode directly echoes *The Fortunes of Richard Mahony*, where the land constantly thwarts the hopes of the settlers, and of Mahony, by the physical vengeance it wreaks on their best endeavours.

Like Mahony, Edward finds the habits of his new associates distasteful. In words that would apply equally to the suburban culture that Bharat and Navaranjini encounter as to the lives of the stockmen with whom he mixes, he describes their cuisine: "The crude cooking of raw, unseasoned meat over burning coals (which passes for the culinary act in these barbarous places) is, for example, something I would find hard to bear during a longer sojourn than I intend to make. The result is often charred, and where it is not so, it is generally raw, the blood still running from it. The smell of it, not to put too fine a point on the matter, is vile." (166)

Previously, he had been able to avoid this crudity because his companion, Davith, had brought with him from Ceylon a "portion of curry leaves, spices and pepper" with which he was able to make the meat "palatable." Yet now, despite his hardships, Edward enjoys the companionship of the stockmen and describes one in particular, Joe, as a "friend" who he hopes "will think of me often with his customary good-hearted kindness." These sentiments bely the truth of the translation he offers of Horace's apothegm: "He who crosses the ocean may change the skies above him, but not the colour of his soul." Edward has already changed, and, although he returns to Ceylon, the liberal breadth he acquires from his colonial experience is, as Bharat acknowledges, (145) the foundation of a family tradition that enables them to explain one culture to another.

While Grandfather Edward's travels are important as precedent and counterpoint, the experience of Bharat and Navaranjini provides the main substance of the book. Bharat, like Richard Mahony, is the intellectual who reflects on his experience, recognizing his alienation, but, again like Richard, he depends on his wife's clarity of understanding to cope with his daily vicissitudes. He recognizes (153) that he lacks the easy acceptance of another culture that characterizes both Navaranjini and Edward. Quite unlike Mahony, he responds to his alienation by strenuous endeavours to become an insider. Central to these is his decision to change his name, so that he and Navaranjini become Barry and Jean Mundy. Yet it is Jean, the more adaptable, who resists this acculturation most violently and effectively, accepting her new name while asserting her native identity.

The issue of identity is central to the fourth section of the novel, entitled 'The Conduct of Travellers.' Previously, Bharat and Navaranjini have been involved in the clash of cultures as newcomers in a strange land. In this section, which looks back on the first five years of their residence, they confront the consequences of their choice. Barry decides that the real moment of his decision to leave Ceylon was when he decided he could no longer endure its confusion. Already largely westernized, he finds an opportunity to make his own choices and adopts the role of cultural communicator. Jean, on the other hand, both remains deeply rooted in her native culture and moves with great practicality into the life of her new country.

At the beginning of the fourth section, Jean, still Navaranjini, decides that Australians, deep down, are really Asians. Their appearance of insensitivity merely conceals their true nature. By acting on this assumption, she breaks through the superficial conviviality of her husband's colleagues to reveal their deeper prejudices, and in doing so discloses her own. The admiration she earns for discomfiting the complacent unrighteous is compounded by her triumph at the university open day, where her exhibition of rare books and manuscripts not only earns a profit for the English Department but confirms her opinion that a common humanity unites Asians and Australians. The mark of this common humanity is the similar and salacious curiosity shown by both parties in a particularly detailed illustrated edition of the Kama Sutra. Encouraged by these successes, Jean accepts the role of supporting her husband while recognizing that she is the one who brings into the new land the old stories that can make sense of the common experience of people of different origins. Similarly, at the end of the novel, when Barry chooses to set up a school to teach English to other newcomers, Jean provides the true meeting point of cultures by establishing a restaurant and school of cuisine. The change of her own skies has changed her soul, and she is now ready to change the skies, or at least the horizons, of her new compatriots.

This ending leaves us with the question of why, although these two novels have a similar structure, the one reaches a comic resolution while the other works inexorably to tragedy. In part, this difference reflects the difference in authors. Gooneratne is an ironist whose principal characters are observers as well as actors in their own stories. This enables them to preserve a distance from events, and so obtain a certain control over them. Those who lack this quality, like the racist Professor Blackstone and the earnest Sri Lankan Australian community leader, Mr. Koyako, are caught in the circumstances they try to manage. By contrast, Richardson is a naturalist whose characters are gripped by a destiny outside their own will. Her novel traces the dramatic irony of circumstance that dooms Mahony to suffer the same fate that he observes destroying others in the early years of his career, and which he foolishly believes he can escape by giving himself to spiritual rather than material concerns.

The personal difference between these two authors however reflects also the historical differences between the times in which they wrote. In the nineteenth century, the fictitious Richard Mahony could no more question the cultural and material supremacy of Britain than could the novelist who, writing in England in the 1920s, through him reproduced the life of her own father. Gooneratne, on the other hand, writes in a time when the imperial certainties of her characters can only appear absurd. Her irony is as much a historical reality as a personal stance. Her achievement is to convert this inevitability of perspective into a declaration of human possibility. Her awareness of the contradictions of culture and individual ambition is contemporary, but her discovery of potential within the contradiction is postcolonial. In recognizing the complex sources of the present, she realizes the hope that these can generate a future, free of the limitations of the past, but not free of the universal absurdities of the human condition. People do, she suggests, change their souls when they change their skies. More importantly, when they change their skies, they do not abandon the past, but produce a new future and new possibilities. These possibilities will determine the shape of the coming Australian republic.

Bushes in Two Hemispheres: A Comparative Study of Susanna Moodie's *Roughing it in the Bush* and Yasmine Gooneratne's *A Change of Skies*

A.G. KHAN

Two women writers belonging to different hemispheres describe the immigrant experience to arrive at different conclusions. While Susanna Moodie's account was to educate the aspirants to not to risk the journey to Canada, Yasmine Gooneratne tries to drive away such apprehensions by asserting that Australia is a place that would not permit one to return home. This paper seeks to study human predicament in two different hemispheres of people caught in adverse circumstances.

II

Roughing it in the Bush[1] was sketched by Susanna Moodie to discourage the ambitious adventurers by narrating the tales of her suffering for seven long years. She did not mince words when she declared, "It should prove the means of deterring one family from sinking their property, and shipwrecking all their hopes." (237) She considered the place "prison house." Her contention was that immigration to such a place would be of little avail to the gentleman because of his peculiar habits and upbringing. "To the poor, industrious workingman it presents many advantages, to the poor gentleman, *none*." (236) The reasons she enlists are convincing—hardships caused by weather and pestilence, treachery of enterprising (but dishonest) adventurers and the connivance of early settlers to rob honest families through mean methods that would trap the gentleman to disastrous investments and soon find himself bankrupt.

Moodie's account is a first-hand account of settlers who brave rough weather and pestilence to reach the shore to find their hopes belied. It becomes an authentic document as the family had spent nineteen years in Canada. The modern text has been considerably edited for a number of reasons that Carl F. Klinck explains in his introduction. (x) Her novel served (at that time) different purposes—for the British, Americans and Canadians. For the Americans it was "a substitute for chivalric romances," for the British it was a source of information on Canada, while for the Canadians it was an account of the country's emergence from blackwood into a land of opportunities, though some Canadians did resent so dismal a portrayal of their country.

"I sketch from Nature, and the picture's true; whatever the subject, whether grave or gay, painful experience in a distant land made it mine own" (xiii) is a befitting introduction to Susanna Moodie's narrative. Realizing that emigration is a necessity (even if an evil) (59-60) "butterfly in a bee-hive" (62) she wanted the readers to apprise of the pamphlets (xvii) that had duped hundreds of people. In an Introduction to the first edition Moodie exposes the myth/propaganda of these pamphlets. "They were made to believe that if it did not actually rain gold, that precious metal could be obtained . . . by stooping to pick it up." (xvii) The obvious result of such false propaganda was mania for Canada who were "easy dupes to the designing land speculators" and thus found themselves into the "snares of their artful seducers."

Susanna Moodie was not pleading a case for the colonists trying to defend them by arguing that the wealth/power they gathered in course of time was hard-earned as a result of constant struggle, perseverance and having undergone risks of several kinds. One should neither envy their gains nor should one accuse them of exploiting the natives. Vassanji's *Gunny Sack* also describes the predicament of those who struggle and earn to be a victim of enterprising people who rob them off the fruits of hard-earned money. To call these people who reach from rags to riches "colonists" is an insult to their patience, perseverance. However neither Idi Amin nor the newly awakened natives accept the fact.

Susanna Moodie does not portray the natives in dark colours. On the contrary, she has all praise for their honesty and sincerity. She finds them neither mean nor quarrelsome. They possess noble qualities that endear them. "The Indian is one of nature's gentlemen, he never says or does a vulgar thing." (25) "People whose beauty, talents, and good qualities have been somewhat over-rated, and invested with a poetical interest. . . . Their honesty and love of truth are the finest traits in characters." (155)

Susanna Moodie's farewell to the backwood is with a touch of sadness because it was there that she could accomplish herself in odd circumstances: "the school of high resolve and energetic action in which we had learned to meet calmly and successfully to battle with the ills of life." (229) She realized that her sufferings made her nobler and stronger, "humble home, consecrated by the memory of a thousand sorrows." (231)

How could one live in so depressing situations? It was Susanna Moodie's faith that was unswerving even in the darkest hour of their sojourn: "the necessity of a perfect and child-like reliance upon the mercies of God . . . never deserts those who have placed their trust in him." (167) There were moments when she lost hope: "The hope which had so long sustained me seemed about to desert me altogether . . . all my courage and faith in the goodness of the Divine father seemed to forsake me." (207) But there is always a dawn after the darkest night: "and hope raised at last her drooping head to regard with a brighter glance the far off future." (215) She was convinced, "a great deal of our distress arose from want of faith." (218)

In addition to faith, humour had its own sunny warmth to clear up the dullness of her life. Moodie sprinkles humour as soothing balm to tone down the gloom. She narrates how Voltaire's History of Charles XII was substituted to serve as Bible for swearing an oath. (21) In the wake of a storm blowing and when every one was feeling miserable the infant in the cradle was also busy "trying the strength of her lungs, and not a little irritated that no one was at leisure to regard her laudable endeavors to make herself heard." (70) Tom's antic with 'old Satan' is equally hilarious. (85) And a tombstone provokes her to question: "Sacred to the memory of silence Shagman . . . was the woman deaf and dumb or did her friends hope by bestowing upon her such an impossible name to still the voice of nature, and check by an adminatory appellative the active spirit that lives in the tongue of woman." (95)

Beginning with picturesque landscape Susanna Moodie's description acquires poetic qualities: "My eyes were blinded with tears—blinded by the excess of beauty—never had I beheld so many striking objects blended into one mighty whole/Nature had lavished all her noblest features in producing that enchanting scene." (22-23) What wonderful combination of beauty and grandeur and power at every winding of that noble river! The St. Lawrence river is described as comprising nature's "grandest elements to form this astonishing panorama. There frowns the cloud-clapped mount . . . the cataract foams and thunders, wood and rock and river combined to lend their aid in making the picture perfect and worthy of its Divine Originator." (29)

Seven years in the backwood began with onslaughts of cholera and ague, climatic furies (106), thefts (170), fire (192) and outbreak of rebellion forcing the only male member in the family to leave wife and children in their sick bed. (209) To add to these natural/man caused miseries 'poverty' was ever present to inflict her tyranny: "As to tea and sugar, they were luxuries we would not think of . . . until I found an excellent substitute for both in the roof of the dandelion." (168) But Susanna Moodie does not curse her misery. On the contrary she even desires poverty: "you must become poor yourself before you can fully appreciate the good qualities of the poor." (217)

A peep into the local customs gives us an idea of "Charivari" in which when an old man married a young wife or vice versa or "two old people who ought to be thinking of their graves enter for the second or third time into the holy estate of wedlock" all the young idle fellows meet together to Charivari them by disguising themselves by blackening their faces and by resorting to much boisterous fun to demand drink or money. (145) Another practice followed is an instance of joining hands together—a cooperative activity (on mutual understanding). When labour was not easily available people used to assist one another in building cottages. Exchange of produce on barter basis or borrowing labour/ox was another method of procuring help.

Borrowing was the most common (and abused) hazard. In most cases it was an euphemism for robbing or cheating because one would never get back the money/article given on loan. Instead of stealing it was given a dignified name—borrowing in which the man who lends remains an eternal loser. Of the various odd characters Susanna Moodie portrayed, many are those who had perfected "borrowing" into an art.

Susanna Moodie gives an excellent account of odd characters she met who made their lives happy (or miserable). Devoting one chapter each to many of them she shows how varied people can be ranging from mean and quarrelsome to compassionate and helpful. Not only do we have sketches of faithful dog like Oscar (35) and a friendship between a pet dog and pig (173) but also an acknowledgement of nobility in the eccentric. Tom Wilson (48-63) faithful and honest, John Managhan (107-16) the ever-complaining Malcom, John (176-91) Mr. E (198) and the maid-servant old Jenny. (209) The early settlers who considered it their privilege or even mission to harass the Moodies by begging/borrowing or stealing are many. Principal among them are Emily (71-74), Betty Frye, Uncle Joe (Old Satan), Betty B who were not only rogues but also rude and arrogant. It is however, necessary to describe two of them in greater details. A very humorous account of eccentricity of Tom Wilson has been given at length: "He is a perfect contradiction. He always laughs and cries in the wrong place." (57) A simpleton among rogues he deserved the prayer, "May God take care of him, for he never could take care of himself." (58) Describing his oddity, Moodie says, "Nature had no counterpart of one who in mind and form was alike original." (51) "This very ugly young man considered himself an Adonis" (50) though his very appearance used to provoke laughter, "the laugh would come—do your best to retain it." (50)

John Managhan, the orphan employed as servant brimmed with vigour, love, kindness and sense of duty. He endeared himself with his stamina for work (109) at the same was ready to risk his life in case of a calamity: "If it's a life that must be sacrificed, why not mine as well as another?" (113) Moodie comments on the travails of such an honest person by making a touching observation: "His whole life was spent in tearing his trousers to repair his jacket." (115)

The two most admirable characters that emerge are Moodie herself and the adorable husband she had. Braving all kinds of onslaught and privation they were "made for each other"—considerate and compassionate to each other. The modern feminist would do well to see how excellently matrimony helped them to tide over storms with cheers. (128-30)

III

In contrast to Susanna Moodie's account of life in the bush, Yasmine Gooneratne's account differs in several respects. First, it is an account moving in time and space. The past century juxtaposed with the present period. Secondly, it also takes cognizance of events occurring at home (i.e. Ceylon) that cast their shadow on the life of people living in Australia—while Moodie had no dispute on any issue, ethnic clashes in Ceylon embittered the lives of Bharat and Baba though removed by a distance of a few thousand kilometers from home. Thirdly, there is only one narrator in Moodie's novel: in Yasmine Gooneratne's there are five narrators—Edward, Bharat (Barry), Navaranjini (Baba alias Jean), Edwina and Moude Crabbe—her canvas is wider, covering several areas.

The common features of the two novels are that both deal with adventures that were catalytic to immigration. They portray the natives in bright colours, never trying to colour their vision with racial prejudices. Though Bharat went to Australia with a kind of ethnic anxiety because of their brown skins and possibility of "Asians Out" "Basha Paki a Day," kind of reception. Their misgivings caused them a lot of embarrassment when they considered Mr. Bruce Trivally's advances as hostility whereas they were courteous and kind to the new emigrants. Their real feelings for the 'brownies' were much camouflaged—something they shared among themselves but tactfully managed to subdue it.

In fact, the hot discussion between Baba and Blackstone over racial discrimination proved to be advantageous and she found in him quite an amiable person. "Australians can be civilized." (128)

Both the novels are autobiographies. While Susanna Moodie's novel is autobiography having sketches of people and accounts of events, Yasmine Gooneratne's novel is a post-modernist work comprising biography, autobiography, newspaper reports and similar techniques employed to suit the narrator or the occasion. While both authors differ considerably in their backgrounds, they share the privilege of being women. Susanna Moodie belonged to a family of gentlemen, her husband having been a soldier for the Queen's cause. Her sisters and their husbands also joined the immigrants whereas in Yasmine Gooneratne's case we have no such information except the fact that she continues to reside in the country of her adoption with her physician husband (while Susanna Moodie returned to England) and is recipient of academic and literary honours. Susanna Moodie had four children; Yasmine Gooneratne has two. Gooneratne happens to be the sole person (till 91) to receive the Doctor of Letters for her literary accomplishments and was also awarded Order of Australia as a recognition of her contribution to literature and education. Susanna Moodie's sisters also made a mark in various fields as did their husbands. While Susanna Moodie's work tells us nothing about the academic, political or social events; Yasmine Gooneratne takes us for a round trip to academic institutions, Radio Stations, Restaurants etc. where we find a more elaborate account of the society not only in Australia but in Ceylon as well.

IV

Edward, the first adventurer in the family of Mudaliyars, chose Australia instead of England which the grandson also opted as visiting Professor of linguistics (a sheer coincidence). Bharat's family had visited England so frequently that settling for anything less than London's Westminster Bridge was a kind of eccentricity. Let us try to fathom how deep are apprehensions and prejudices about Australia among people at different places.:

> There's nothing there . . . just Kangaroos and sheep. (18)
>
> Totally uncivilized. No idea how to dress or behave in someone else's capital city. (18)
>
> White Australia policy. (19)
>
> . . . a nation of uncouth drunks, with the intellectual standards of a TV soap opera and the social standards of the football scum. (134)

Even the Australians do not have much pride for their land because of their allegiance to England. We are informed, "Australians have been living in a time warp . . . fixated on the mother country." (29) The decision to spend five years in Australia was considered a kind of cultural *harakiri* as it is a "cultural desert" and chances of being "sucked into a great emptiness" were predicted.

To make matters worse the early immigrants who have been reaping rich dividends in the new country, instead of assimilating, try to project a scarecrow impression. Over-reacting to local situations, he tries to overplay the "ethnic identity" tune.

Mr. Koyako, shortened from Mekaborn, Kiyanhati, Balapan, Koyako, feels that his allegiance to his motherland can be expressed only by growing "a luxuriant moustache" in the style of Sri Lanka's first Prime Minister, constantly carry "a camera in imitation of her second" and so on. (89-90) What a ridiculous show of one's loyalty! Since children are likely to be 'contaminated by' the casualness (92) he advocates people to conscientiously keep up all their national customs. (93) Such persons always raise hoax about their insecurity—social, economical, or political (93) or else they would become "bottom dog." (94)

Complaining about Australians' habit of shortening long names, Mr. Koyako's name for example—'almost a short story' (97)—as a proof of their laziness is because when written they take up all the available space on paper or "air-space" on radio/TV. 'Creuzoither' becomes 'Crew,' 'Padapopoulos' becomes 'Pad.' Hence, in course of time, Bharat became Barry and Navaranjini is shortened to Jean. To Mr. Koyako this was a loss of cultural-identity. It is because of this, the Australians fail to remember people by names but by their professions as is evidenced by repeated reference to Bharat as "Dr. What's-his-name." (98, 99, 100) The natives also have double standards. In their personal estimate they rate immigrants and their songs/music quite poor. Hence music on 'Zither' (Sitar) couldn't be called music, "cats on roof tops, cats on tiles, cats with syphilis, cats with piles." (100) Similarly, the red velvet dot between her eyes (stick on) is confused with the third eye of Shiva. (101) With a warning that it might 'scare the horses,' (101) upset by absence of wall to wall carpets they regard cushion "culture" with pity/envy! However, while dealing with these immigrants, they wear a facade and begin praising everything exotic. Interest in "Kamasutra" also prompts them to "stoop" to Asians for their expertise. (197)

Bharat appreciates the Australian's ability to love and respect others. He could sense, "Australians are true Orientals at heart." (117) They might seem a bit rude (or indifferent) but "Australians hide their sensitive souls under a rough exterior." (117-18) Hence if people regard

"Australia, the most dangerous country in the world" little realizing the fact that "Australians never had an empire." (118) The racists might label Asians "ching-chong" (119) but aren't "we Asians racist about colour" (119) argues a discerning Bharat. Asians, he'd said on radio, "pollute the air with the fumes of roasting meat. And we Australians . . . must be alert to the dangers involved for our society if we allow Asians in who cannot assimilate and accept our customs." (121)

Hence being practical Bharat and Navaranjini became Barry and Jean while their family name Mangala-Davasinha was reduced to "Mundy" lest the "suit" should be confused with a Sikh! "Barry scrapped his spectacles and went in for contact lens" (125) is a symbolical shift of saying good bye to one's old perspective of looking at life from an Asian's "spectacles." He was quick to realize, "she doesn't like immigrant mynahs and immigrant crows. But she thinks kindly of *us* as exotics who are having difficulty in sending roots into alien ground." (87)

Bharat's pragmatism was based on sheer commonsense, "Australia is a wealthy country in which the sheer volume of waste . . . can surely merit being rewarded." (143) Apart from this Barry wanted to interpret his culture to the Aussies. (145)

What distinguishes Asians from Aussies is their approach to work. Because of abundance there is an apathy towards work (189, 190) as has been explained: "The Aussie weekend ish six daysh long." (192) The novel forces us to realize the unpleasant realities of Asia. On this point it echoes what Bapsi Sidhwa's protagonist in *An American Brat* feels. There is no "Home" because it is no longer peaceful nor warm. Foreign stay in fact creates a kind of contempt for people at home for their myopia and apathy or indifference.

Compared to Susanna Moodie's work who does not describe what was happening in England meanwhile, Yasmine Gooneratne is all the time aware of the conflicts and chaos prevailing in Sri Lanka (and unfortunately even today in more violent outburst). Hence the disenchantment in *A Change of Skies* is total.

"Sri Lanka is not our country now Barry," (306) felt Jean. Her daughter rightly observes: "The magic gone . . . the beggars are crooks and conmen—Asian reality's a long way from your pretty Raj films. . . . That the elephants on the islands have been practically killed off now, that the tea estates are run down—that the pretty smiling village girls out there are toting Kalashnikov AK 47." (318, 319) It is ironical that the man who had been vigorously "acting" during his entire stay in Australia returns to Ceylon to become Minister for the Arts, Cultural Affairs and Tourism being only a propagandist imitating all the past

Prime Ministers in one way or the other while Bharat who had been really trying to recuperate himself with ideas and visions of "home" should die uprooted.

"Writing Great Grand Dad's biography was for Dad a way of going 'home' even if it was only in memory and imagination." (321) Australians visiting Sri Lanka in search of 'real' land fail to realize "comedy exists in Real Sri Lanka" (24) though they know well in advance "holy places in the East simply stink." (25) Hence for Bharat and Navaranjini, the Colombo after their return was an "unknown" place (235) in wake of political insurgency taking heavy toll of lives every day, (243) making one "long to be back in Sydney (263) because the landmarks of Colombo are no longer the same. "It's four houses down from the third rubbish heap after the traffic lights." (263)

While Susanna Moodie's book was meant to be a guide to prospective immigrant to Canada to discourage him and stay home; Yasmine Gooneratne's book develops a nausea for home thus encouraging him to return as early to Australia as possible. The contrast in Kandy described on page 26 is quite sharp to one on page 265: "Kandy is just so wonderful—it's the Real Sri Lanka" (26) whereas we find "Insulation from experience" (265) in order to conceal the Real Sri Lanka. "The history of colonial occupation and international bullying. Picturesque as it is, I find it quite easy to live without it." (270)

V

Immigration during the nineteenth century is the highest common factor between the two novels. Moodies went to Canada in the middle of the nineteenth century, so did Edward in 1890 to Australia. And therefore the hazards of weather and pestilence are common. Death taking a heavy toll of immigrants in both, the countries "only 11 from a party of 32 survived the misery" (164) the land filled with agonizing cries of "Badagiri/Badagiri" (165) for help. For them a return to home was salvation. "He who crosses the ocean may change the skies above him, but not the colour of his soul." (167)

Asia that Yasmine Gooneratne wants to de-construct/de-colonize must not be "depicted as diseased . . . the leperous pale patches." (238) Hence Edward succeeds in having a memorable "Return." Strangely, like Edward, Edwina too is trying to shake herself clearly off the colonial burden. While Bharat and Navaranjini had to get their names swapped and get recognized as Barry and Jean, Edwina redeems her past by turning the clock back and from Edwina she becomes Veena because while Edward smacked of colonialism with the name of King Edward the Seventh, Edwina was after the last vicerine of India. (318) In this way, the Empire strikes back.

Another common feature of the two texts is their bright and kindly humour. Both Susanna Moodie and Yasmine Gooneratne can laugh at feminine frailties. If Susanna Moodie could portray eccentric characters like Tom Wilson we have in Yasmine Gooneratne Mr. Koyako described with immaculate precision an extremely odd person. (89-90)

The two books can also be studied in terms of synchronic linguistics—English in the nineteenth century in Canada vis-a-vis in Australia. While English in Canada was quite close to the Victorian excellence, in Australia it was struggling to find a proper pidgin. Shortening as shd, wd, cd, we have a taste of Australian English (of 1999) when we are told that "bastard" is a term of endearment. (121) "Make all your chooks turn into emus—and kick you flaming dunny down." (129)

While Susanna Moodie had no qualms in portraying herself as the shadow of her husband, Yasmine Goorneratne portrays Jean differently: "she stopped being Dad's shadow and struck out a line for herself." (321) Her feministic concern is eloquent (though in a subdued tone). "Women abos, gays, kids, koalas, druggies wholes, and now the Asians, endangered species every one of them." (131)

Yasmine Goorneratne follows the techniques and jargons of deconstruction/post-modernism. Journey/voyage motives along with field notes are mentioned. The narrators are writers—writing becoming a springboard for narration—Edward wrote a diary; Bharat a Guide; Baba a book on cookery; Edwina her field notes. The past and present, similarly Australia and Sri Lanka, are juxtaposed. There is shuttle cock like movement of narrators.

The two novels, when read together, afford an excellent understanding of the different lands, people, cultures and predicaments.

NOTES

1. Susanna Moodie, *Roughing it in the Bush* (Toronto: McCelland and Stewart, 1987).
2. Yasmine Gooneratne, *A Change of Skies* (New Delhi: Penguin Books India, 1992).

Miles Franklin's *My Brilliant Career*: A Feminist Perspective

MADHURI CHATTERJEE

Miles Franklin is recognized as the founding member of the Australian literary canon, though she lived for a significant part of her adult life outside Australia. In his monograph on Franklin, Ray Matthew suggests a parallel thematic concern as *My Brilliant Career* with other female writers including Mary Hays and the Brontes. He states, "I have mentioned the Hays novel because Miles Franklin a hundred years later, a hemisphere away was in a similar social position." The narrator in her 'autobiographical' novel is a girl in a man's world—a girl who 'being so very plain' knows herself 'not a valuable article in the marriage market.' This world offers her nothing respectable but the slavery of teaching or her slavery of marriage."[1]

The novel is a bildungsroman concerned with the maturation and education of her heroine but Franklin consciously adopts a masculine pseudonym to reveal her deference to the aesthetic world that acknowledges male superiority. Michael Foucault believes power structures to be dynamic and not usually repressive yet it checks the potential power of woman. They voice their concern only through writing which are sometimes distorted and become the "curse of weakness."[2] It is very conspicuous in *My Brilliant Career* where the culture denies full aesthetic liberty to the writer. As a woman writer Miles Franklin also lacks a literary model or a cultural identity.

The novel is the story of Sybylla Penelope Melvin's childhood and adolescence, her initiation into the patriarchal world, her conflict and finally her self-discovery. The bond of marriage as a financial and economic contract disturbs the narrator early on in the novel, "Grannie dead old grannie, thought that I should marry a man who from a financial point of view has a good match for me. That is where the sting came in. No, I would never marry. I would procure some occupation in which I could tread my life out, independent of the degradation of marriage."[3] The novel stresses more on this degradation with the partner as an equal participant to it. Sybylla dreams of economic independence but her ambition for a brilliant career is vaguely defined and appears "boundless as the mighty bush." (33) Marriage on the other hand becomes the "goal" (11) of life, culminating in the girl's growth and expectation. Hence, Sybylla dreams of a feminist utopia where women will be self-sufficient and not dependent on the male: "why did not social arrangements allow a man and a maid to be chums . . . enjoying each other without thought beyond pure platonic friendship. But . . . the conceit of men." (69) Sybylla's negation of marriage stems from the treatment her Aunt Helen had received. She regards her aunt the paragon of woman but the lady is abandoned and psychologically destroyed by a male. After marriage she is cast aside for a mistress and hangs in a feminine limbo "neither wife, widow, nor maid." (49) The two views reveal not only her conflict and tension but also reflect the social and economic condition in Australia.

The narrator convincingly struggles with the male values—accepting and denying them. She tries to reject her femininity and strongly identifies herself with masculine qualities—initiative, adventurousness and courage and looks at mateship as sexless bonding. She even flirts with Frank Hawden, her other suitor and casts off her marriage ring and "unwomanly" strikes the male. But soon, she has to reject all her positive beliefs and deep feelings and blind her weary life to female expectations. Her tone "I am only a woman!" reveals her self-denigration and self-congratulation and focuses the textual shift from romanticism to realism, from happiness to misery, from affirmation to apologia. In a way *My Brilliant Career* attempts to portray the subversion of women in a society which allows the women to grow only in its own reductive terms. Sybylla's attempts to enter the masculine world leads only to greater ambiguity and confusion.

A sense of subordination and domination persists in the novel's heterosexual relationship and authority is imposed with the image of the whip. The narrator Sybylla is first confronted with pain when she comes across a black snake and though her father rescues her by "dispatching the reptile with his stock-whip, he had been smoking and dropped his pipe on the ferns. I picked it up, and the flowing embers which fell from it burnt my dirty little fat fists." (2) Later submission is forced on her through whip, when Harold Beecham attempts to kiss and tame her: "He cracked it round and round my head and arms, but I did not feel the least afraid. . . . It was thanks to Uncle Jay-Jay that I was able to bear the operation with unruffled equanimity, as he was in the habit of testing my nerves in this way." (77) Masculine power and authority bears down on feminine complacency and leaves Sybylla's "white arm and shoulders—so susceptible to bruises—many marks and black." (148) She is also torn between two worlds—marriage is forced upon her by the grown ups and her refusals lead her to punishment and reward as imposed on a child.

The duality within the novel is also portrayed through the image of the mirror. The mirrors of the house are all turned around for a period of time, when Sybylla laments her lack of beauty to her aunt. Later she is allowed to look into the mirror in a correct way only when she is dressed in an attractive feminine manner. The narrator once again raises the point that a girl has to be acceptable to males before she is acceptable to herself. The self-denigration which Sybylla suffers each morning because she is not pretty, leads to a deeply damaged psyche. She realizes:

> As a tiny child I was filled with dreams. . . . As I grew it dawned upon me that I was a girl—the makings of a woman! Only a girl!—merely this and nothing more. It came home to me as a great blow that it was only men who could take the world by its ears and conquer their fate, while women metaphorically speaking were forced to sit with tied hands and patiently suffer as the waves of fate tossed them hither and thither, battering and bruising without mercy. Familiarity made me used to this yoke; I recovered from the disappointment of being a girl, and was reconciled to that part of my fate. In fact, I found that being a girl was quite pleasant until a hideous truth dawned upon me—I was ugly! (33)

Her inability to accept a positive role constantly challenges and restricts the narrator, reinforcing the ironic duality that the restrictions are placed not by society alone but by women themselves, who act as conspirator of their own race. The novel also reflects the psychic and emotional deprivation of male-dominated culture. Sybylla is punished and condemned by fate to lead a life of unremitting, unrewarding toil. The societal conditioning imposes upon her the accepted pattern of behavior of subordination-domination, victim-conqueror and leaves her insecure.

In the novel, the dominant patriarchy is revealed and a sense of self-discovery is finally attained after much feminine protest and rebellion. Miles Franklin's biography also suggests that feminine movement formed an integral part of her personality and as woman she "constituted a subculture within the framework of a larger society unified by values, conventions, experiences and behaviour impinging on each individual."[4] In the long tradition of women's writing, *My Brilliant Career* is a text which has successfully attempted to raise many feminine statements.

NOTES

1. Ray Matthew, *Miles Franklin* (Australian Writers and Their Work Series, Melbourne: Landsdowne Press, 1963), p. 9.
2. Virginia Woolf, "Women and Fiction," *Women and Women Imagination* (The Women Press, 1979), p. 47.
3. Miles Franklin, *My Brilliant Career* (Australia: Angus Roberston Classics, 1974), p. 72.
4. Elaine Showalter, *A Literature of Their Own: British Women Novelists from Bronte to Lessing* (London: Virago, 1978), p. 13.

Humour in Elizabeth Jolley's *My Father's Moon*

K. RADHA

Elizabeth Jolley, one of the best known women writers of Australia, was born in the industrial Midlands of England in 1923. She came to Western Australia in 1959 with her husband Leonard Jolley and three children. She had studied nursing in London during 1940-43 and in Birmingham from 1943 to 1946. She has had a wide variety of occupations including cultivating a small orchard and teaching part-time at Curtin University of Technology. She was honoured with an award for her contribution to Australian literature not long ago. In addition to fiction she has also published poetry in Australian journals and anthologies, which, together with her plays, have been broadcast on British and Australian radio. She has to her credit three collections of short fiction, and nine novels, of which *Mr. Scobie's Fiddle* won "The Age" Book of the Year Award, *Milk and Money* the NSW Premier's Award, and *The Well* the Miles Franklin Award. Her first collection of stories *Five Acre Virgin* (Fremantle Arts Centre Press, 1976) has most of the characteristics of her long fiction. Her novels, according to John McLaren, "combine a gothic interest in the extraordinary with a capacity for depicting ordinary life on the margins of Western Australian society. Her work places issues of female sexuality, including lesbian relationship, in the context of the universal struggle to survive and establish patterns in life. Her characters encompass retired schoolteachers, cleaning women, nurses and a range of misfits. They have in common an insecurity, a need to belong, that gives them both an off-centred view of society and a need to find a stake of their own within it."[1]

In many of her works the contrast between the need for security and the desire for freedom is well brought out. It has been truly pointed out that "The hallmark of Jolley's writing is irony, even fantasy, so beautifully controlled that the reader is shunted between the pitiable, the hilarious, and the profound in a quite dizzying way . . . Elizabeth Jolley joins the handful of Australian writers . . . of whom it may be said that their books are able to alter the direction of one's inner life."[2]

This paper is a very personal response to Jolley's novel *My Father's Moon*. The title reminds us of a phrase in Browning's "My Last Duchess," "everybody's moon." It is not a long novel; it has only 171 pages but its length is quite deceptive. One should not think that one can finish reading it in a couple of hours. No. It is a short but very complex novel. For a book of its size there are too many characters. The narrative technique is somewhat confusing as that of Golding's *Free Fall.* The story in brief: Veronica Wright, a Quaker known as Vera to her relations and friends and called Nurse Wright officially in hospital, is the chief protagonist (heroine or anti-heroine). During wartime she goes for nursing after six years at school and she falls in love with a married doctor, Metcalf. He goes to the front and is killed (there are different versions about his death). Vera gives birth to a daughter and after trying at many jobs, when her daughter Helena is five, she leaves her home—at that time both her parents are alive—to work in a school where they can live, and Helena can be educated. But she is disgusted with the people there—all perverted—and the poor food she gets. So she decides to leave the school a few days later. Meanwhile her father whom she loves more than her mother, passes away. Her only hope lies in Miss Ramsden, whom she had known as a senior staff nurse at the hospital. She writes to her but she is not sure whether her address is the same. She leaves the school, Fairfields, with Helena and gets down at a bus terminus where she has requested Ramsden to meet them. But Ramsden does not turn up. Perhaps the address which Veronica has is more than five years old and Ramsden may have changed her residence. Veronica waits for her in vain. A policeman takes the mother and the child to the night shelter. There the woman in charge gives them food and bed. Veronica asks the woman if she knows a Ramsden. She remembers only one thing—Sister Ramsden had gone to Mombassa with the Queens Nurses, nothing more. The story when narrated, as I have done, may look very simple. And one may be disappointed with the story content. Even an "uncommon" reader will have to read the book several times to make out the story and unravel its complexities. The book is divided into twelve chapters: Fairfields, My Father's Moon, Recha, Bathroom Dance, Night Runner, Lois, The Hunt Gertrude's Place, Ramsden, Single Malt, Diet Kitchen. It is perhaps not the story, but the other aspects which make this book unique and worth reading.

The novel is full of humour even though the theme is pathetic. One of the major aspects of the novel which will impress the reader is the tendency of the protagonist to compare persons and places—typical of women. On going to school she says: "Almost at once I began my game of comparisons, placing myself above someone if more favourable and below others if less favourable in appearance." (31) Before meals at school the children have to stand in line beginning with the smallest and ending with the tallest. During this time of silence and inspection by the prefects Veronica makes her comparisons. She compares her defects with those of her immediate neighbours.

> I glance sideways at the pleats of their tunics and notice that the girl next to me bulges. In my mind I call her Bulge; her pleats do not lie flat, they bulge. She is tall and awkward, taller than I am and more round shouldered. I try to straighten my back and to smooth my tunic pleats. I can be better than Bulge. She has cracked lips and she bites her nails. I try not to chew my nails but my hands are not well kept as are the hands of the girl on the other side of me. She has pretty nails and her hair is soft and fluffy. My hair is straight but not as greasy and uneven as Bulge's. Fluffy Hair's feet turn outward when she walks. My feet are straight but my stockings are hopelessly wrinkled and hers are not. We all have spots. Bulge's spots are the worst, Fluffy's complexion is the best. She is marred by a slight quint. We all wear spectacles. These are all the same except that Bulge has cracked one of her lenses. My lenses need cleaning. (32)

Bulge's real name is Muriel. Sometimes Veronica suffers from an inferiority complex. "I wish I could be small and neat and pretty like Amy, or even quick like Helen Ferguson who always knows what's for breakfast the night before. . . . I do not have this quality of knowing and when I look at Helen Ferguson I wonder why I am made as I am. In class Helen Ferguson has a special way of sitting with one foot slightly in front of the other and she sucks her pen while she is thinking. I try to sit as she does and try to look as if I am thinking while I suck the rounded end of my new pen." (34) Later she compares her mother with Bulge's mother. "If I compare my mother with Bulge's mother it is clear that my mother is below Bulge's mother in the comparison. My mother has never had a pet of any kind." (129) "Because of being above Bulge in my comparisons at school, her hair, her cracked spectacles, her complexion and the way in which she stood, bulging and biting her nails, everything being worse. I do not especially like thinking about her. This thinking puts us on the same level." (130) "In my secret game of comparisons Bulge was placed high up, far higher than anyone else, for she had the school doctor at her bed in the night. I was envious and felt ashamed of being envious and tried to be helpful." (132)

The game of comparison is continued at the hospital too. (102) In the anaesthetic room she watches Sister Snorter entering with her hair not combed properly. "Her theatre gown has no tapes at the back so that it hangs untied and crooked. She only has one boot on. . . . The unfairness of it all comes over me. Why do I have to be neatly and completely dressed at all times." (59) The anaesthetist Mr. Porter, according to Veronica, has something of her father's voice. But she cannot "compare" with Sisters Diamond and Snorter. "I like Snorter's clothes and wish that I had some like them." (53) Her own coat is very "ugly" and her blue skirt is "too long, the material is heavy, it sags." (53) Diamond is very pretty and Snorter, "horsey." Looking at Magda and Metcalf, Veronica thinks thus: "The bodies of rich people are always suntanned and handsome. . . . People like me are always white. . . . My face is gaunt with the dark circles of night duty for ever round my eyes." (125)

Veronica is sometimes capable of mischief. She is good also at lying and stealing. She is thus a typical "anti-heroine" if I may use the term she can be the female counterpart of Jim Dixon in Kingsley Amis's *Lucky Jim* and Charles Lumley in John Wain's *Hurry on Down* or to mention a real person, Dylan Thomas.

Lying is an art and Veronica does it exceptionally well. Miss Ramsden wants to visit Veronica's house. But as Veronica's sister is ill there is not enough space for Miss Ramsden. Veronica meets the senior nurse at the station and tells her: "I'm most awfully sorry but there's been something of a tragedy at home" (4) and Ramsden decides to go back. The following morning she lies to her mother "She wasn't on the train." (5) Of course this is a harmless lie. Veronica buys a ring for six pence. But she pretends that it is for "a drama, for a play in dramatic society." "I'm in a play, er Shakespeare." (169) Perhaps when Veronica realizes that she is pregnant she wants to pass for a married woman. As she is not well off, she can afford only a cheap ring. At a school meeting on one night when Bulge is weeping the Matron tells Bulge that she would have a hot bath and some hot milk in half an hour, Veronica does not go back to the Meeting but has a hot bath and manages to get the milk from the maid who gives it to her by mistake, as her bed is nearer the door. (38)

Whenever a young nurse commits a mistake or misbehaves or there is urgent matter to be discussed, she will be asked to meet the Matron at nine a.m. To have her vengeance on Staff Nurse Sharpe who always makes her work hard, Veronica pulls out the laundry baskets, buckets of water etc. from their normal places. When Sharpe and an auxiliary nurse Queen go along to the lavatory they fall over these things and knock into each other, making the biggest disturbance ever heard in a hospital at night. Both the nurses are asked by Night Sister Bean to report to Matron at nine a.m. (68) The nurse Helen Ferguson and others go out with men saying that Veronica has no sex appeal (S.A.). When the Night Sister Bean enters the room, Veronica tells Helen that all the men are talking about her and that Corporal Smith, who is married, is absolutely mad about her because of her sex appeal. Sister Bean overhears these statements and asks Helen Ferguson to go to the Matron at nine a.m. The mischievous Veronica wakes up Corporal Smith at four a.m. and urges him to write to Nurse Ferguson. (70) Veronica keeps Corporal Smith's love letter to Ferguson, sixteen pages, in her pocket. Helen's name does not appear anywhere in the letter. "It is too long for one person. So I divide the letter in half and address two envelopes in Corporal Smith's handwriting, one to Sharpe and one to Ferguson." Accidentally she drops them unsealed, one by the desk in Night Sister Bean's office and the other in the little hall outside Matron's room. (74)

On another occasion when Nurse makes Veronica do some of the most disagreeable work, she goes into the small ward and gives the emergency bells three rings. Sister Bean thinks that it has been done by Sharpe and Queen. They are to report to Matron's office at 9 a.m. Moreover, they have been smoking on duty.

The Home Sister is in the habit of leaving notes in the nurses' rooms. On Ferguson's dusty dressing table she reads the note telling Ferguson to clean her hair brush. Veronica whose handwriting is so like the Home Sister's, adds, "Neither a Borrower nor a Lender be." When Nurse Sharpe is in the letter queue, she takes the loaded ash tray from the Porters' Lodge and spills it all over her room. She leaves a note: "Your room is disgusting. Take some hot water and disinfectant and wash down sister." (71) When Sharpe is in the letter queue on an earlier occasion, Veronica rushes to her room and crams her curtains into her messy wet soap dish and leaves one of her neatly folded notes on her dressing table: "Do not let your curtains dangle in the soap dish, sister." (71)

Veronica is an adept in stealing too. If at school she cheats Bulge of her milk and hot bath in hospital, as a nurse she moves a step further. She lifts large quantities of milk powder, soup, chicken and other things. "In the pantry, I am opening a big tin, the biggest thing I have managed to lift out so far," (69) she says. She occasionally carries home milk powder and chicken to her mother! There are many instances of her loading herself with tins of tomato soup, chicken, sardines and milk powder.

The novel would have been very gloomy and morbid but for incidents like these. There are several other situations which contribute to the humour and at times to the irony in the novel. At Fairfields, Mrs.

Olive Morris, a poor and hardworking woman with three children, is visited by her husband, Mr. Morris. Veronica does not know that he is a criminal wanted by the police. He impresses every one with his talk at supper. He makes them think that he is the perfect husband and father. He gives all sorts of presents. (16) But to everybody's surprise he is soon taken away by the police in handcuffs for he has a long stretch of prison life ahead. Later Patch, Miss Palmer, the Principal gets bills addressed to her for all the presents from Mr. Morris!

The umbrella of Veronica's father also contributes to the humour in the novel. He always carries his umbrella with him and at the railway station waves goodbye with his umbrella. He also uses his umbrella to point out the sun or the moon in the sky, causing embarrassment to his daughter. He loses his umbrella in trains and it travels the length and breadth of England, coming back at intervals, labelled from Liverpool, Norfolk, St. Ives, and Glasgow to the lost property office where he will be with a kind of apologetic triumph, able to claim it. (26) There is Helen Ferguson's mother who puts laxatives in the puddings she makes. (46) We have the lady in charge of the night shelter who when asked about Ramsden tells Veronica the story of the cook's murder in Mombassa where Ramsden had gone. Veronica comments, "Perhaps the cook in Mombassa was often murdered horribly in these attempts to provide answers." (29) Ferguson reminds Vera of the white sauce she made at school which was said to have blocked up the drains for two days. Her pastry board, put up at the window to dry, was the one which fell on the headmaster's wife while she was weeding in the garden below, breaking her glasses and altering the shape of her nose forever. (55)

One night Veronica hears two voices in the adjacent bathroom and when she peeps through the key hole she sees Diamond and Snorter quite naked singing and dancing a minuet. Then they climb into the deep hot bath and tenderly wash each other. When they meet again the next morning, Veronica mischievously tells Snorter: "Minuet du Salle de la bain" in her appalling accent. (59) Thus the novel though morbid abounds in humour.

NOTES

1. *Australian Literature: An Historical Introduction* (Melbourne: Longman Cheshire, 1989), p. 234.
2. Qtd. from *Washington Post Book World* on the back cover of *My Father's Moon* (Victoria: Viking, 1989).

The Theme of Entrapment in Peter Carey's Fiction

M.D. FLETCHER

In an important analysis of "postcolonial" writing, Ashcroft, Griffiths and Tiffin have argued for the centrality of metonyms to that enterprise. Postcolonial writing in "settler" countries Australia, Canada, New Zealand, the United States has differed from its counterparts elsewhere. In Australia in particular, the theme of entrapment or imprisonment—reflecting white Australia's origins as a penal colony—has been a major metonym.[1]

Throughout Carey's fiction, both literal and figurative entrapment are invoked; and while naturally one must be careful not to see figurative entrapment everywhere, Carey is usually quite overt in that respect. His fictions abound with actual prisons and cages, which perhaps serve as metonym for Australian society. But he also is fascinated by the construction of entrapping structures, as Graeme Turner reminds us,[2] and often that involves individual, figuratively entrapping structures.

Carey has indicated in an interview that *Illywhacker* marks his attempt to come to terms with Australia,[3] but many of the themes and motifs of *Illywhacker*, and of *Oscar and Lucinda*, are anticipated in *Bliss*, including that of imprisonment or entrapment, and in this essay I look at some of the ways in which that theme is deployed in those three novels.

As Laurie Hergenhan notes in his *Unnatural Lives: Studies in Australian Fiction about the Convicts*, Foucault has changed our thinking about imprisonment by demonstrating how its characteristics permeate other modern power relations.[4] The similarity between prison and an asylum is the most obvious point, but, in addition, the ability to observe unseen provided by the panopticonic design of Bentham's reformed prison heralds a transition to self-surveillance and what Foucault calls the "capillary" surveillance of social self-surveillance or surveillance by the whole society rather than by outsiders from above. Carey depicts a number of these themes in the three novels discussed here.

The major protagonist in *Bliss*, Harry Joy, is literally taken into custody by the police and later committed in an asylum. Harry also sees himself as literally trapped in Hell, and the terms "trapped" and "prisoner" are employed by Carey to describe other situations in the novel as well. Hassall, in particular, has suggested that Harry's wife Bettina and children David and Lucy are depicted as "trapped in the socially approved roles he [Harry] has imposed upon them," while David and Bettina and Bettina's lover Joel "are trapped in other people's stories and kill themselves."[5] In addition, Harry and his employee, Alex Duval, are similarly trapped in marriage, in advertising, and finally in the asylum itself.[6] Some of these points seem questionable, while others require elaboration.

Bettina's desire to become a "hot shot" in advertising has been thwarted by Harry's refusal to bring her into the business, and his expectations and perceptions of his children do not correspond to reality, but the imagery of entrapment is not prominent in those cases (although David seems entrapped in his own romantic fantasies).

Hassall's comparison of Alex and Harry is more telling, however. Carey is explicit in describing the game in which Alex's wife is able to trap him time after time, even having him released from the sanctuary of the asylum for that very purpose, and he is inventive in creating the nightmare which embodies Alex's experience of that entrapment. Similarly, while Harry does not initially feel trapped in his own marriage, he is certainly ensnared in the deal with Bettina that secures his release from the asylum.

Harry is trapped in the city and in advertising by his love of comfort, just as Alex is trapped in the dishonesties of advertising by his fear of losing his livelihood. It is appropriate, then, that after Alex is mistaken for Harry and committed in the asylum, Harry is in turn committed and in effect "becomes" Alex. Alex already has the name Harry Joy when the real Harry arrives, and once re-labelled the real Harry begins to act like Alex.

Hassall's third point, that those who are in someone else's story (Bettina, David, Joel) kill themselves, also warrants extension. In this context it may be illuminating to compare Harry's trip to the police station with his incarceration in the asylum. He is taken to the police station for driving an unroadworthy vehicle after a circus elephant sits on his little red Fiat. He finds himself close to serious trouble because his story is the retelling of an old joke and totally implausible. Although he is manhandled by the arresting officers, he manages to tell an original story, and although there is not even a pretence of relevance to the condition of his automobile, he is released.

In the asylum, on the other hand, Harry has no more stories to tell.

Although he tries to follow Honey Barbara's advice and avoid the double bind of claiming persecution and thus opening himself to the diagnosis of paranoia, he is trapped in the warders' definition of reality, even "becoming" Alex once he is assigned that name.

Finally, the theme of people being entrapped within certain perceptions of reality also is carried by Harry's belief throughout most of the novel that he is imprisoned in Hell. In a conceit reminiscent of Don Quixote, Harry believes he is in Hell and that actors are playing the roles of this family and acquaintances to fool him. His imposition of that frame influences his interpretation of events to confirm his perceptions, and his actions on that assumption even create responses from others that re-enforce his suspicions.

In *Illywhacker* the forms of imprisonment once again are literal as well as figurative. The story begins with Herbert, the "Illywhacker," telling the story of his life and that of his family. In mid-life Herbert spends a long period in gaol. In Herbert's terms, being in gaol forces him to shrink, to assume a character that does not attract attention or retribution and even to become physically shorter, leaving him permanently changed. Compare, from *Bliss*, Harry Joy's stay in the asylum, where he begins to take on the actual personality of Alex Duval.

Before being gaoled, Herbert had enjoyed travelling about the countryside with Leah. After leaving gaol he is re-united with Leah, now freed from caring for her invalid husband, but he no longer has much to offer—he simply wants to be taken care of by his family. A high level of self-surveillance is employed to adjust to conditions in gaol, and the experience of gaol carries over into civilian life as a continuing state of reduced expectations.

In another sense, however, these characteristics were present in Herbert as a young man. *Illywhacker* is about lying, and the liar may be entrapped as well as liberated by lying. As Helen Daniel argues, from the very beginning of his relationship with his wife, Phoebe, and her family, he becomes trapped in his own lie about the snake he has with him—that it is a pet, a lie designed to impress Phoebe—and causes her father's death in the process of attempting to substantiate his lie.[7]

Daniel also suggests that Herbert's marriage to Phoebe does not last because Phoebe flees "the cage she perceives as Herbert's life."[8] More specifically, Herbert, orphan that he is, is continually building homes to create a family, from which Phoebe flees as she attempts also to escape from the entrapment of having children, as she equates Herbert's idea of home and family with prison.[9] In this sense Herbert as a young man anticipates Herbert as an old man looking for a family in which to be cradled.

The story of Herbert is paralleled by the story of his son, Charles, and Charles' wife, Emma. In his youth, Charles is trapped at the Chaffey farm for months during a drought. Les Chaffey has taken apart his motor bike, and Charles cannot leave until it is reassembled. This episode results in Charles and Emma meeting, however. Once married, Charles and Emma happily manage an enormous pet emporium, but the turning point in their story occurs when Emma begins to live in one of the pet cages after a misunderstanding with Charles.

Ultimately, the emporium is refinanced with Japanese money as a human display emporium for tourists. The theme of colonization as imprisonment, and of indigenes seen as exotics on display, is clear here. The denouement is anticipated not only by Emma's taking up residence in a cage but also by Herbert's desire to be taken care of like a pet. Even before the emporium is re-organized for the display of humans, Herbert has been observed at the window of his room between letters of the pet shop's neon sign, similar in effect to the bars of a cage or prison cell. In a final (or perhaps initial) twist, Herbert was already giving his spiel from the beginning of the book from inside the human pet emporium, despite giving the impression at the outset of being an independent raconteur.

The theme of imprisonment in *Oscar and Lucinda* is carried somewhat differently by the two title characters. Lucinda finds the entire world a prison, entrapped in the conventions and expectations of her society "even without [the] whalebone and elastic" that she refuses to wear.[10] She is even admonished to shorten her stride, failing to wear the conventional clothing that would inhibit it automatically and compare Honey Barbara in *Bliss*, whose stride is contrasted to the hobbled walk of city women and who strikes David as disconcertingly "wild and untrammelled."[11]

Inadequately socialized as a woman (according to her mother's mea culpa), Lucinda must be kept in her place by the gaze of men in groups and by the Foucauldian "capillary" surveillance of everyone—the lawyer, Ahearn, the glass blower, Phelps, and even her maid, Mrs. Smith—admonishing her to stay within accepted boundaries.

Oscar, on the other hand, experiences a series of prisons of various types. Throughout the novel he is entrapped in his religious belief, making a series of extremely painful and important life decisions on the basis of throwing lots or flipping coins. Travelling to Australia from England by boat, he is trapped below deck by his fear of water, and has to be hoisted onto the boat initially in a cage.

Working in a room full of clerks for d'Abbs, Oscar is subjected to the "panopticonic" oversight of Jeffris, under which everyone works silently even though there are no articulated rules. During the journey to the outback with the glass church, he is literally Jeffris' prisoner, and is confined to a wagon designated "the Ladies Compartment" to add to his ignominy. Finally, of course, he dies entrapped in the glass church as the river water rises through cracks in the glass and the door to the church jams.

Oscar and Lucinda together conspire to construct an entrapping misunderstanding as elaborate and cleverly constructed in its way as the glass church itself. As in a classic romance, they deepen the misunderstanding in a minuet of steps, the difference being that the classical romantic resolution fails to occur. Lucinda eventually prays for Oscar to release her from "the prison her foolishness had made for her," (410) but divine intervention is not forthcoming.

Lucinda, afraid that Oscar will think she has him in mind for marriage, pretends to a continuing and exaggerated passion for Hasset well after he has left her life both physically and emotionally, including keeping letters on the mantelpiece, so she will not lose Oscar's company altogether. When she thinks he might be ready to reciprocate her interest in him, convention as well as the fear of appearing too bold hold her in check, and she waits for Oscar to speak first.

Oscar is crushed by her deception concerning Hasset, as he loves her already. He fears revealing his love for her, lest she be offended and withdraw or even refuse to see him. Indeed, assuming himself to be in competition with a clever, "manly" Hasset, Oscar sees his only hope as appearing to be saintly—as unselfishly good and, of course, not pressing his suit. His Christianity compounds this approach, leading him to hope that self-sacrifice may be the road to desires fulfilled.

Lucinda and Oscar conspire, then, to invert each others' meanings to maintain the edifice of misunderstanding. They enter into the wager of whether or not Oscar can deliver the glass church to Hasset in the outback by Palm Sunday, which ends in his journey into the heart of darkness with Jeffris and his death trapped in the glass church.

NOTES

1. Bill Ashcroft, Gareth Griffiths and Helen Tiffin, *The Empire Writes Back: Theory and Practice in Post-Colonial Literatures* (London: Routledge, 1989).
2. Graeme Turner, "American Dreaming: The Fictions of Peter Carey," *Australian Literary Studies*, 12:4, October 1986, p. 435.

3. "Peter Carey, Interview with David Sexton," *Literary Review*, 84, June 1985.
4. Laurie Hergenhan, *Unnatural Lives* (Brisbane: University of Queensland, 1983).
5. A.J. Hassall, "Telling Lies and Stories: Peter Carey's *Bliss*," *Modern Fiction Studies,* 35:4, Winter 1989, pp. 645, 639.
6. *Ibid.*, p. 646.
7. Helen Daniel, *Liars: Australian New Novelists* (Ringwood: Penguin, 1988), p. 171.
8. *Ibid.*, p. 173.
9. Peter Carey, *Illywhacker* (Brisbane: University of Queensland Press, 1985), p. 205.
10. Peter Carey, *Oscar and Lucinda* (Brisbane: University of Queensland Press, 1988), p. 251.
11. Peter Carey, *Bliss* (Brisbane: University of Queensland Press, 1981), pp. 203, 211.

Parodying the Picaresque in Peter Carey's *Illywhacker*

M.D. FLETCHER

Peter Carey's intention in *Illywhacker*[1] is to expose Australian pretensions. Genre is important to intention, and I argue in this essay that *Illywhacker* can be read as a parody of the (already parodic) picaresque form, as part of a broader postcolonial reading.[2] As one clue to how this novel might be read, it invokes Thomas Berger's *Little Big Man*, itself a parody of the genre of the American western, ostensibly narrated by a 111-year-old man with incredible blue eyes and of questionable veracity.[3] In *Illywhacker,* Herbert Badgery, the "illywhacker" of the title, claims in the first sentence to be "a hundred and thirty nine years old"; in the second paragraph he tells us: "I am a terrible liar and I have always been a liar," (11) and slightly later it is revealed that he has eyes of "the clearest, coldest blue." (26)

Lies and lying are central to this novel, both Herbert's lying and the more serious cultural self-deception that it mirrors and exposes. Carey says in an interview that his purpose is to expose as lies two underlying assumptions of Australian culture—that the country was empty when the whites arrived, and that contemporary Australians are independent spirits.[4] But the picaresque or another parodic form would serve that purpose. The additional level of parody, parodying the picaresque itself, may attack the Australian claim to self-perception and an ability to laugh at ourselves, undermining the Australian larrikin tradition.

Picaresque novels generally feature the somewhat repetitive adventures of a single, travelling main character who survives on his cunning by imitating life around him. In this way the picaresque exposes social and political corruption and degeneration by reflection. Deception is central, while secondary characteristics include orphan status, suspicion of romantic commitment as entrapping, and the picaro's delight in his own cunning often combined with superficial repentance.[5]

The picaro is unaware of his own defects, and the narrative is generally limited to the narrator's perspective as autobiographical remembrance, thus exposing the picaro as well as the society he reflects. These narratives often adopt and invert the chivalric romance and parody the travelogue or confessional (for which trust in the author is paramount).[6]

Ronald Blader and Marvin Gilman, in particular, have analyzed *Illywhacker* as picaresque.[7] As they indicate, Herbert's mother dies when he is young and he leaves his father while still a child, so that he is effectively orphaned; the entire book constitutes his autobiography; he is mobile, selling automobiles, flying aeroplanes and travelling around; as a salesman he lives by prevarication, revealing lying to be the great Australian pastime; he is irresponsible, permanently losing his daughter in the woods in an act of carelessness[8]; and he moves through experiences without learning or changing.

In addition to these picaresque characteristics as identified by Blader and Gilman, it is worth noting a number of additional points. One is the very centrality of lying and the need to give it additional emphasis here as it relates to Herbert's cunning. His cunning is updated from traditional picaresque to include such ploys as securing a commission job selling automobiles when he first arrives in Geelong so that he can meet the local newspaper editor in a new Ford, or being able to write advertising copy that will attract an audience to entertainment that is honestly entertaining but difficult to sell honestly.

Primarily, however, his cunning involves prevarication. Naturally, everyone around him also lies, except his son Charles, about whom he says, "with Charles the truth was an obsession. I don't know where it came from." (386) Even Honest Leah becomes Lying Leah. (395) Herbert reflects the atmosphere around him, realizing in fact that people only appreciate his company when he tells lies. (79) He also lies to get things done and, occasionally, simply for the enjoyment of it or because he cannot help himself (120, 50), and he cannot clearly distinguish between lies and stories. But his lies are white compared to the lies in official information and recorded history.

The second point is that Herbert also fails at romance. Romantic expectations build up in a traditional manner, with Leah and Herbert reunited after years of separation due to her caring for her invalid husband and Herbert's term in gaol, but their reunion is an anti-climax. Initially he does not recognize her, and ultimately he loses interest. He is unlike traditional picaros in that he has children, but his romantic liaisons do not work.

The third point is that, picaro-like, Herbert is unaware of his own defects. While he is conscious of his lying, he does not realize how selfish and difficult he is to live with, simply proceeding with his own projects that impinge on everyone (e.g. restructuring Charles' living quarters cum pet shop, 541) and plagiarizing Leah's work. (548-49)

In addition to its picaresque characteristics, however, *Illywhacker* also parodies the picaresque. Even the truthful nature of the title—indicating that Herbert is an illywhacker or confidence man—inverts the picaresque tendency to ironic titles, such as *The Good Soldier Svejk*. Herbert not only survives by lying in the text, in true picaro manner, he also lies as narrator, thus upsetting the picaresque form. He immediately challenges the reader with the liar's dilemma[9] by stating that he lies about everything, and then compounds the issue by saying that he lies about everything except his age, which we know he has lied about. (11)

Indeed, Herbert is a false picaro. First, despite his picaro-like failure in romance, Herbert is far too charming, handsome and generally attractive to women—notwithstanding his picaro-like bowed legs (188)—for a real picaro. Second, Herbert evidences considerable self-recognition. Not only does he realize his own propensity to lie, he also recognizes how easily he fools even himself: "[When lying] I was so enthusiastic that I could convince myself in half a sentence." (27) Third, this apparently independent worldly-wise raconteur who begins the book regaling us with his stories, is in fact from the outset in the human zoo that the Japanese eventually make out of Charles' pet store. This may be deception by omission.

Finally, Herbert is hardly a true picaro. For Phoebe, his first wife, it is love at first sight because Herbert arrives by aeroplane and she is ready to fly, but he only wants a conventional family life, exercising his passion for building and expanding homesteads. Leah has revelled in the travelling snake and magic show, and looks forward to a romantic reunion with Herbert, but he simply wants to relinquish responsibility for himself. He has been diminished by his time in gaol, where he successfully attempted to shrink (physically and psychologically) to avoid notice, but his behaviour near the end also links to his pre-prison search for family. As he has said of a time when Phoebe has left him and his mother-in-law takes care of him: "Oh, how pleasant it is for a man to be looked after, and if I have made myself a pitiful thing, a broken spirit, an invalid with no dreams left, I do not take it back but present to you the other side of the grubby coin: that year with Molly when I did not need to strive, to impress, to make a sale, to do anything other than sit in the sun or by the fire." (333)

In conclusion, then, Herbert does not have even the independence of a picaro. In this reading, not only has Australia failed to achieve political and cultural independence, even the Australian male's symbolic independence from domesticity, embodied in the concepts of swagman and larrikin,[10] has been parodied, as Herbert is much more "domestic" than any of his female counterparts. Even the pseudo-independence of refusing to take one's dependence seriously is undermined.

NOTES

1. (St. Lucia: Univ. of Queensland Press, 1985).
2. For the broader postcolonial analysis, see M.D. Fletcher, "Peter Carey's Post-Colonial Australia I: Illywhacker: Lies, Dependence and Political History," *Australian Political Ideas*, ed. Geoff Stokes (Kensington: University of New South Wales Press, 1994).
3. Thomas Berger, *Little Big Man* (London: Eyre & Spottiswoode, 1965).
4. "Peter Carey, Interview with David Saxton," *Literary Review*, 84 (June 1985).
5. See especially Christine Whitbourne, ed., *Knaves and Swindlers: Essays on the Picaresque Novel in Europe* (London: University of Hull, 1974); M.D. Fletcher, "Satire: Purpose, Traditions and Context," *Contemporary Political Satire: Narrative Strategies in the Post-Modern Context* (Lanham: University Press of America, 1987).
6. Barbara Babcock, "Liberty's a Whore: Inversions, Marginalia, and Picaresque Narrative," *The Reversible World: Symbolic Inversion in Art and Society* (Ithaca: Cornell Univ. Press, 1978).
7. *Roguery: The Picaresque Tradition in Australian, Canadian and Indian Fiction* (Sydney: Butterfly Books, 1990), pp. 55-60.
8. Presumably she disappears down a mine shaft, as Blader and Gilman suggest, but compare also the traditional (Frederick McCubbin) style of Australian landscape painting, in which people are almost invisible; Anne-Marie Willis, *Illusions of Identity* (Sydney: Hale and Iremonger, 1993), pp. 81-83. Compare also the manner in which women are invisible in the Australian bush myths.
9. See Helen Daniel, "Lies for Sale: Peter Carey," *Liars: Australian New Novelists* (Ringwood, Vic.: Penguin, 1988), pp. 145-85.
10. This connotation has attached to the concept of the larrikin, despite the original use of that term to designate street hoodlums. James Murray, *Larrikins* (Lansdowne Press, 1973). There is in addition a tie between larrikins and picaros in terms of the ambivalence between criminality and mere mischievousness attached to each; picaros, like larrikins, have been conceived of as "delinquents." E.g., Dorothy Jones, "Larrikins and Termagants," *Thalia*, X:2, 1989.

Mandala Symbolism in the Novels of Patrick White

SHAIK SAMAD

Patrick White views all intellectual activity in Australia with a sardonic eye. The inner hollowness of Australian life is felt intensely in his fiction. Greatly disturbed with the spiritual incapacity, which he calls bitterly "The Great Australian Emptiness,"[1] he appears to be determined to make an effort to help the Australians to become a race possessed of understanding. The characters in his novels enact this aim. He relies almost exclusively on the intuitive process to create the experience of illumination, and it therefore becomes an intensely poetic and personal experience. Most of his characters suffer deeply in order to arrive at self-knowledge.

White conveys "a splendour, a transcendence, which is also there, above human realities" through the "juxtaposition of images and situations and the emotional exchanges of human beings."[2] He could not accept the sterility, the vulgarity, and in many cases the bigotry of the Christian churches in Australia. He abandons the church and evolves images and symbols of his own to worship.

White appears to have succeeded in finding a suitable objective correlative for his emotions in the Mandala image which he uses as a pattern as well. It has been suggested that White draws on Jung for his circular images of perfection, which Jung calls mandalas. Jung explains the mandala thus: "Mandala, a Sanskrit word, means circle or magic circle. Its symbolism embraces all concentrically arranged figures, all circular or square circumsferences having a centre, and all radial or spherical arrangements."[3] He adds that the mandala is divided into a light and a dark half, and when it is employed in ceremonies it always has great importance, because it "contains at the centre a figure of the highest religious significance: either Shiva himself—generally embracing the Shakti—or Buddha, Amitabha, Avalokiteshvara, or one of the great teachers of Mahayana. Or it is simply the Dorje, the symbol of the union of all the divine powers, whether of a creative or destructive nature." (128)

The Mandala, to White, is similar to Jung's explanation: "The Mandala, is a symbol of totality. It is believed to be the "dwelling of the god." Its protective circle is a pattern of order super-imposed on psychic chaos. Sometimes its geometric form is seen as a vision (either waking or in a dream) or . . . Or danced."[4] White shares with Jung a common interest in the Mandala as a traditional symbol of unity and arrives at a similar understanding that the experience of wholeness, of the union of opposites, of reaching a point above conflict, is also an experience of God. White recognizes mandalas as signs of the divine pattern of the world.

The mandala image has a universal cutting across the confines of one particular country or religion to figure prominently in ancient as well as current practices all over the world. As Patricia Morley points out:

> The Mandala image, although frequently cited as an oriental image of perfection, has its place in the Christian mystical tradition, as in Dionysius use of the circle as an image of the outgoing of all being from God, followed by its return. The mandala is also prominent in Christian art, in the radiant halo of light surrounding the heads of divine personages. God is described as sitting upon the circle of the earth, and walking in the circuit of heavens. (Isa.40:22; Job 22:14)[5]

She further remarks that White uses the mandala as an all-inclusive anagogic metaphor "throughout his work to suggest the infinite and eternal living body in which man has his being, the symbol which unites all other symbols, the word that contains all poetry." (17) While Cynthia feels that White's images of trees, flowers, sun, water, glass marbles, hats, tables, and chandeliers, acquire the significance of mandalas,[6] White himself says: "I suppose I begin in some cases with a central symbol—the Chariot or the Mandala, for instance."[7]

White's images fuse sharply into each other so that the mandala emrges as the single image common to all the experiences and is present at the time of illumination of most of his visionaries in the novels.

In *The Living and the Dead*, White experiments with that mandala which develops out of a configuration of geometric forms. He uses the image of cocoon-like boxes which become box-like rooms to mirror the relationless existence and deathly isolation of Standish family. Each character is imprisoned in his own box-like room. It is Elyot's childhood experience at Ard's Bay, a peaceful circular basin of water, that gives him a feeling of security and solidity, and recurs in his memory several times, always with the connotations of ultimate significance. The cocoon-like box or box-like room, the gla box presented by Connie Tiarks and the quaternary of Standish family, which all have a simliar geometrical pattern of a square, ultimately become one box and are juxtaposed to the Chinese boxes, which are spherical like the Ard's Bay. In China the box typifies concord and harmony. In Chinese Buddhism, it is one of the eight emblems of good luck, a symbol of wholeness. It corresponds to the yang-yin principle, identical with the Sanskrit lingam and yoni and the mandala which has both the male and female aspects of the living world. White juxtaposes the Chinese boxes to the square glass box to contain the conflict between those who live by intuition and those by reason. At the end of the novel, Elyot rejects the square glass box, leaves the square cell of his room and walks off to Victoria station's fiery hub. He realizes that man-cosmos relationship is one of the totality of human relationships which determine the deeper quality of human life. He accepts the drunk as a part of himself.

The Aunt's Story is concerned with Theodora's quest for the inner self. One of the unifying images of the novel is Meroe. Meroe spells out peace and completeness for Theodora. It is a symbol that has multi-faceted meanings. Not only is it a natural part of the Australian landscape in spite of its exotic name, its description indicates that functional architecture meets with White's approval, which suggests a mandala. It is a circle with no beginning or end, divided into two distinct landscapes. On the north side are the pine trees, a clear masculine symbol in this novel which is closely associated with George Goodman, father of Theodora. In direct contrast to this bit of uncultivated wilderness there is the rose-garden, expensively, almost artificially maintained by Mrs. Goodman. Then, where are the trees so dead that they seem abstractions of trees, which conform to Theodora's fluctuating sexual identity. The landscape in Theodora's final journey in America, approximates to this in shooting at the red eye of the hawk, Theodora destroys a part of her own self. It is in the Jardin Exotique section that the great monster self is destroyed. Finally, she accepts the 'irreconcilable' halves. Theodora puts on a large hat with a black rose trembling on it. The rose is a mandala symbol indicative of her newly won wholeness.

The ramifying imagery of a spreading tree provides the ideal controlling pattern of *The Tree of Man*. Stan Parker's quest, as reflected in the title, "is not progress along a road or way but growth. And the way is inward, coil by coil, towards the central core."[8] Actually, the tree is a mandalic image. It "denotes the life of the cosmos, consistence, growth, proliferation, generative and regenerative processes. It stands for inexhaustible life. . . . It corresponds to the Cross of Redemption and the Cross is often depicted, in Christian iconography, as the Tree of life."[9]

The Tree of Life is a standard Biblical symbol, but White is almost as familiar with the Kabbala as with the Bible. The Kabbala helps to understand the novel even better. The Sephirotic tree has two aspects, one benign and the other, the reverse side, malign. On one side are the Sephiroth, on the other, the dread Olippoth. Since the Kabbalists consider man to be a macrocosm, the double-natured tree is a picture both of the universe and of the human mind, whose faculties, even the lowest, can work for good or ill. If one looks into one's heart, one will see the holy aspect of the tree. The tree also symbolises "the dual nature of Gemini, the parallel worlds of living and knowing. Jung affirms the bisexual nature. He confirms the unifying significance of the cosmic tree. (332) It is interesting to note that White is a Geminian.

The image of the tree is in a completely organic relation with the story of Stan and Amy Parker, the representative man and woman. Their story and the novel begins and closes with trees. Stan Parker's life leads him finally into the centre of a mandala. Through this image of mystical circle, his final state of inner unity and perfection is conveyed. He is one with nature when he believes in the leaf and the cracks in the path. He discovers God in a gob of spittle. He recognises that "One and no other figure, is the answer to all sums."[10]

In *Voss*, Voss seeks perfection which is "always circular, enclosed."[11] The desert and the comet are the mandalic images. The image of the mandala is used, here, as a framework comprising the land and the sky and Voss is placed at the centre of it. For Voss, a journey through the landscape results in a journey to the core of his true inner self. His relationship with the landscape passes the physical bounds and enters the metaphysical realms. The wilderness provides him a chance to understand not only the power of God but also the state of the individual soul. He achieves humility and simplicity in the west desert when he sees the circular comet. For Laura, knowledge comes through the sufferings she undergoes in the country of the mind.

The fiery Chariot and its four riders in *Riders in the Chariot* symbolize the mandala and the quaternary, which suggest wholeness. In the novel, the Jewish faith is repeatedly represented as a "closed circle,"[12] one lit up by the love of God. The round table, the geometric carpet and the wedding rings of Reha and Mrs Godbold are mandalic. Each of the four principal characters shares a vision of the riders in the chariot, a highly personal one for each, yet something which unites them, transcending the confines of culture, race and religion. Himmelfarb sees God in the table and feels that all creation encapsulates sparks of divine fire. Mary Hare identifies closely with the earth she loves and becomes part of it in the end. Mrs Godbold sees wholeness in the service of others. Dubbo's paintings are his acts of worship.

The mandala attains fullness and solidity in *The Solid Mandala*. Here again, we have the mandala and the quaternary as the two dominant images. There are four parts in the novel, four epigraphs, four characters, four corners to Arthur's dance and four marbles. Arthur's four solid mandalas provide another link between the square and the circle. It refers to quaternio or the quadratura circuli, which, in alchemy indicates completeness and perfection. Moreover, White makes use of the twins to represent the two halves of the mandala. The twins, both brothers, who are two halves of one personality, are essentially complementary to each other. Arthur, finally, achieves self-realization in the whirling patterns of his dance.

The Chandelier of the Courtney house in *The Vivisector* acquires the significance of the mandala. It represents the artist's Mad Eye and his power to express its vision of truth and beauty. Hurtle Duffield comprehends art as an avenue to a realization of the "Divine Vivisector,"[13] God, and both the successive women in his life and his paintings represent stages in his quest for a perception of pure being. There is a circular movement in their relationship. Life cycle itself has a circular movement. Hurtle Duffield achieves the final oneness, unity of the artist and the work of art, as he paints the vertiginous blue before his death in the studio.

Both 'the Eye' and 'the Storm' in *The Eye of the Storm* are mandalic and symbolise the cosmic drama significantly linked with the life of Elizabeth Hunter. Ortiz observes that the hurricane, like celestial bodies, has two characteristic motions: rotary and sideways. In its sideways motion, there is an intermediary point of absolute calm: the so-called 'eye of the hurricane.' For American aborigines, the hurricane is cosmic synergy, since it contains three elements within itself namely, fire-or-light-rays, air or wind, water or rain, and disturbs the fourth—earth. It was worshipped as deity of the winds and waters, and also of the heavens. This aspect brings us once again to the celebrated and persistent celestial symbol of the 'hole' in the disc of Chinese jade, representing the concept of the zenith as a void through which one may pass out of the world of space and time into spacelessness and timelessness.[14] Elizabeth Hunter has her moment of enlightenment by a storm-tossed sea. The relation of timeless spiritual reality is achieved at the still centre of the storm. She goes back to it at the moment of her death.

The dominant images in *A Fringe of Leaves* are: a fringe of leaves, the wedding ring, the storm and the St. Hya's well. Like every closed circle they all allude to the mandala. Ellen Roxburgh undergoes a searing but spiritually illuminating experience after her shipwreck off the Queensland Coast. She is stripped of her social position, possessions and even clothes, until she is reduced to wearing a vine round her waist—hence the 'Fringe of Leaves'—to hide her wedding ring. The illumination that Ellen Roxburgh is vouchsafed is garnered piecemeal during her sojourn in the forest and not in one dazzling moment like Elizabeth Hunter. Ellen, finally, attains a vision of unity in Pilcher's rude chapel.

In the last novel, *The Twyborn Affair* the wheel comes full circle. White uses the image of androgyne to work out his ideal of making oneself whole, of making a mandala of one's life. Eddie Twyborn lives three lives as Eudoxia-Eddie-Eadith, representing the transformation from female to male to female. The hermaphrodite, suggestive of wholeness, corresponds to the mandala, and tends to converge so as to create a vast anagogic perspective. Eddie attains wholeness when he dies in the woman's make-up in the bombardment, while Eadie Twyborn's instant of enlightenment is woven into the garden in her mind.

It is thus attempted to establish that the mandala image is central to any understanding of the religious vision of Patrick White.

NOTES

1. Patrick White, "The Prodigal Son," *Australian Letters*, Vol. 1, No. 3 (1958), pp. 37-40.
2. Thelma Herring and G.A. Wilkes, "A Conversation with Patrick White," *Southerly*, Vol. 33, No. 2 (1973), pp. 136 and 138.
3. C.G. Jung, *The Integration of Personality*, trans. Stanley Dell (London: Kegan Paul, Trench, Trubner, 1940), p. 58.
4. Patrick White, *The Solid Mandala* (Harmondsworth: Penguin, 1969), p. 238.
5. *The Mystery of Unity: Theme and Technique in the Novels of Patrick White* (Montreal: McGill Queen's Univ. Press, 1972), p. 234.
6. Cynthia vanden Driesen, "Patrick White and the 'unprofessed factor': The Challenge before the Contemporary Religious Novelist," *Patrick White: A Critical Symposium*, ed. R. Shepherd and K. Singh (Adelaide: CRNLE, 1978), pp. 83-84.
7. Herring and Wilkes, p. 140.

8. Patricia Morley, p. 103.
9. J.E. Cirlot, *A Dictionary of Symbols*, trans. J. Sage (London: Routledge and Kegan Paul, 1962), p. 328.
10. Patrick White, *The Tree of Man* (Harmondsworth: Penguin, 1974), p. 477.
11. (Harmondsworth: Penguin, 1960), p. 198.
12. *Riders in the Chariot* (Harmondsworth: Penguin, 1964), p. 103.
13. (Harmondsworth: Penguin, 1973), p. 259.
14. Cited in J.E. Cirlot, pp. 147-48.

Text and Meaning: A Deconstructive Analysis of Patrick White's *Voss*

D.N. BANDYOPADHYAY

Voss is supposed to be based on the true record of Ludwig Leichhardt who died in the Australian desert in 1848.[1] In this novel, White presents a mysterious German figure who attempts to overreach the untoward circumstances of life by trying to cross the Australian continent for the first time.

It has been sometimes interpreted as a novel with a significant epical dimension. In fact, traditional epical properties put forward in the context of a modern design are not hard to find. It is possible to locate certain proximate patterns of parallelism between the traditional epic of Homer and Patrick White's *Voss*. It may be pertinent, therefore, to chart out the points of parallelism:

Iliad	*Voss*
1. Assembly of the Achaean soldiers.	1. Voss's collection of certain expeditions' adventurers.
2. Vastness of the epical battle.	2. Vastness of the journey.
3. Difference between Achilles and Agamemnon.	3. Difference between Turner and Voss.
4. Achilles' withdrawal with the Myrmidons.	4. Withdrawal of Turner and others with Judd as the leader.
5. Laocoon and the snake signifying a decisive finality.	5. The Great Snake and Voss.
6. Final pessimism in death and destruction.	6. Finality reached through a series of deaths.

But this parallel design seems to be an artificial construct that is carefully devised only opting out certain significant dissimilar factors.

Whatever epicality there may be in the design, it does not, apart from its expansive vastness and sublime elevation of human experience, fulfil the required epical arrangement.

But a closer reading of the text unfolds a radically different layer of meaning. In fact, it is strictly relevant to depend on the given 'word,' the 'signifier,' to reach the point of true 'meaning' or the 'signified.' It is again the rational correlation, to that extent, of the text and the meaning that may help us to reach a proper explanation of the novel.

II

'People of that kind will destroy what you and I know.'

The idea of meaning is almost coterminous with knowledge. For the science of meaning itself signifies a system of knowledge.

The modern quest for knowledge begins to take shape in a different direction with Edmund Husserl's phenomenological philosophy that considers the world as a reflection of consciousness: and speech is an expression of absolute meanings that exists separately from language. Husserl's phenomenology holds further that pure meaning exists first as a pre-verbal transcendental signified and then finds expression through human voice. But this critical position comes to be totally challanged by Jacques Derrida's ideal of desconstruction that stands firmly against Husserl's critical principle insofar as Derrida questions the latter's belief in the pre-linguistic absolute meaning. Derrida finds a difference or division within the sign between its two aspects. In other words, he discovers an infinite range of variables in the inter-relationship of signifier and signified. Thus the signifier 'Nature' may suggest a large number of possible signifieds. Again, all these possible signifieds in themselves become signifiers suggesting another series of signifieds; and this process may continue *ad infinitum.*

Signifier	Signified	Signifier
Nature	1. Character	Identity Type
	2. Essence	Purity Ultimate
	3. Substance	Matter Solidity

Thus Derrida's post-structuralist notion of deconstruction finds fault with the absolutist ideal that confines meaning to a limited boundary. Derrida visualizes an open-ended, infinite possibility of meaning that underpins an appropriate perspective of modern explication. It is to be differentiated from the structuralist denunciation of historical and biographical criticism. By ignoring other layers of information from traditional history and biography, the structuralists ran the risk of ignoring the creative author in the context of specific historical/social/economic perspectives. They as a result only concentrated on the written word and canvassed the principle of absolute meaning. But Derrida's philosophy of deconstruction seeks to get away from this systematic contradiction by preparing a striking hermeneutics of interpreting a text with reference to a large number of possible variables.

It seems that Patrick White's *Voss* exactly corresponds with a deconstructive pattern through a large number of explications intended in the text itself. He has, therefore, marked a sharp break with the traditional story arrangement and interplayed a terrible expedition with the normative design of life. Again frequent intrusion of visions and telepathic correlation presents a collapse of traditional realism. If we prepare a gist of the story pattern, it seems to be surprisingly slight. We come across Voss, the Germen explorer, in the house of Mr. Bonner with the explicit purpose of crossing the Australian continent. Here he collects fellow-adventurers, develops a mutual feeling of love with Laura Trevelyan and makes for the disastrous journey. Then follows an alternate pattern of Voss's progress and the reactions in the house of Mr. Bonner, with a distinct stress on Laura's love-lorn waiting. It ends up with the cleavage within the party and consequent death of Voss and others in the desert. Things are rounded off with the discovery of the mysterious conditions of Voss's death and Laura's prospective hopefulness.

Voss has been presented as a figure who stands opposed to steadfast, fixed meanings. He, in fact, considers the deconstructive method of destroying the normative limitations of meaning. When Mr. Bonner seems doubtful of the results of the expedition and asks, "You are aware, I should say, what it could mean?" Voss replies, "If we could compare meanings, we would arrive perhaps at different conclusions." (20) Even the figure of Voss himself is deconstructed by means of interactions of other characters. When he refuses to dine with the Bonners, different perspectives of the man come to surface: "A rude man saw Mr. Bonner. A foreigner, saw the P.S. Someone to whom, after all, I am completely indifferent, saw Laura Trevelyan." (24)

Even in matters of primary discussions on the mapping out of the journey, there is concentration on open-ended indeterminacy. When the fellow journeymen try to present a slapdash dependence on a fixed purpose, they come to feel that there is no strict purpose. Le Mesurier ironically says: "purpose? So far, no purpose." But Voss perfectly realizes the nature of variability that goes antithetical to determined meanings and purposes. Voss reflected, "I would be purposeless in this same sea." (33) Again Le Mesurier seeks to substantiate an idea of codified routine by asking the time of the expectation. This once again breaks down by Voss's rejection of formulaic codification: "One mouth, Two mouths. It is not yet decided." (35)

The moment of their journey in a ship has also been conceived in terms of multiple reactions from the standpoint of involved spectators. Voss and the party set sail in a ship called 'Osprey' which has become almost a symbol of a macrocosmic world in a strange, infinite microcosm. The entire picture once again comes to be deconstructed through variant attitudes of three women. For Laura, it is an escape out into a broad prospective world: "Yes, they have not got away." (121) Rose Portion feels inclined to pray for the explorers: "Oh, I will pray for them." (121) Belle suddenly waxes eloquent on Palfreyman's nicety, quietude, education and kindness. But such scattered, disjointed opinions come to be merged into a deep sense of melancholy. Thus the essential impact finally yields a larger dimension of inexplicable sadness: "Their bodies shivered in their thin gowns; their minds were exposed to the keenest barbs of thought; and the whole scene that their vision embraced became distinct and dancing beautiful but sad." (122)

The cave experience of the explorers equally point to the range of flexible variables. The cave with its rock drawings not only indicates a sense of shelter but a sense of mysterious interior that creates a design out of an apparent formlessness. But the experiential mode of all this has been deconstructed by the interpretative variety of the reaction: "The simplicity and truthfulness of the symbol was at times terribly apparent, to the extent that each man interpreted them according to his own heeds and level." (279) But the deconstructive variants finally lead up to a distinctive foreshadowing of Voss's death at the end. The picture in the cave, therefore, seems to point at a linear teleological movement: "See, this man is going to die. They have planted a spear in his heart. It has gone in at the back through the shoulder-blades." (280)

III

'Tempus fugit'

The spatio-tempora relationship comes to be a significant contributing factor to the idea of deconstruction prevalent in the novel. It can be expressly meaningful in the context of a teleological perspective. In *Voss*, we are often led to look backward and forward: backward to the past and forward to the future; and this movement of time naturally coalesces with the progress in space. It can be said to approximate a linear design that deconstructs the idea of the present through a demonstration of the past and the future.

Consider, for instance, the first meeting of Voss and Laura. After initial formalities, both of them refer themselves to the past. Laura finds herself "threatening to disintegrate into the voices of the past." (12) For Voss equally "the past now swelled in distorting bubbles." (13) The stray, half-forgotten, silhouetted moments of past establish a new meaning of their totality. Finally Laura's invitation to see the garden (Chapter I) foreshadows the garden incident when they come to be co-sharers in the participation of mutual love (Chapter 4). The garden episode in its turn again transcends the limited unit of time to move forward to a vision of future. Laura and Voss are "faced with a great gap to fill, of space, and time." (68) They come to discover in a deterministic way that "future is will." (68) The consciousness of future again and again torments them because of its inherent uncertainty and mystery. Laura comes to be saddled with the pressure of an internal indecision: "The future? Laura Trevelyan could not bear to think of it, even though the present, through which the riding party moved, was still to some extent an unpleasant dream." (119) The entire novel seeks to grasp the phases of past and future that finally conduce to an epistemological understanding of life and existence. This explains the pithy conversation of Mr. Ludlow and Laura. When Ludlow asks: 'When does the future become present?' Laura curtly responds: 'Now.' Ludlow gets extremely puzzled and Laura explains: 'Every moment that we live and breathe, and love, and suffer, and die.' (447) Ludlow seeks immediately to concretize it with reference to Voss's death. But Laura gets beyond the limited frontier and strongly affirms a linear prospective ideal of life: "Voss did not die. He is there still, it is said, in the country, and always will be." (448)

There is also a co-extensive pattern of dream, vision, hallucination and even primitive cults that help the deconstructive process of thought. In fact, the pattern of realism comes to be again interrupted by moments of extra-realistic visualization. Palfreyman's precise reaction to the sailor's inexplicable story of guilt and romance perhaps sums up the entire idea: "You wished to live what you dreamed." (17) For all practical purposes, dreams take on the shape of a vision and hallucination. When 'Osprey' sets sail, Laura comes to be absorbed in a persistent dream and sees the vision of the "whole rows of sailors blackened teeth gaping from a tunnel." (119) Again during the mystical experience in the cave, the idea of the snake ritual comes to be uppermost. The black fellow refers to the King Snake that is a symbol of a father figure: "Father my Father, all black feller." (274) It is the snake king that visits Le Mesurier in his dream. He finds himself wrestling with the "great snake, his king, the divine powers of which were not disguised by the earth-colours of its scales." (281) The ominous vision of the snake comes to be concretized towards the end of the novel when Voss stoically waits for the final moment of death: Jackie enacts the story of the Great Snake and Voss anticipates the approach of the gradual progress towards death.

This has been again curiously mixed up, through an inexplicable suggestion, with Laura's mysterious fever. There is a sporadic assemblege of cult-tokens like dew gathering,[2] (339) the snake symbols, the appearance of a comet, "the odious pears" which present forth a seminal crisis. The crisis for Voss through a division in the party and the approaching death at the hands of Jackie comes to be paralleled by Laura's undiagnosed mysterious fever. This finally reaches a level of mystical experience when Laura in a sort of delicious dream promises to Voss: "I shall not fail you. Even if there are times when you wish me to, I shall not fail you." (358) This comes to be alternately repeated in Voss's vision of Laura and is further mystified when he exactly visualizes Laura's sickness, her strangeness and beauty: "Then he looked at her, and saw that they had cut off hair, and below the surprising stubble that remained, they had pared the flesh from her face. She was now quite naked and beautiful." (367)

IV

'Voss did not die'

White's novel, thus deconstructed, should however lead up to a significant, perceptive conclusion. Deconstruction, as always, through a presentation of large number of uncodified variables expand the perception of knowledge. This central force is also at work through the hermeneutics of signifieds. Thus Voss is sometimes an ordinary man, sometimes an explorer, sometimes a foreigner, sometimes a leader and sometimes even equable with God. Laura is also a woman, an intellectualized idea, even a dream. These variables are posited in terms of a number of relationships in the context of the normative world.

The journey of Voss and the inner development of Laura finally yield a process of gradual transition from being to becoming. In the garden episode, Laura simply looks upon themselves floundering "into each other's private beings." But this shades off into an acceptance of life as a continuum that grows, develops and finally embraces the finality of life. Thus during the cave experience, Voss states: "The mystery of life is not solved by success, which is an end in itself, but in failure, in perpetual struggle, in becoming." (71) It is this process of becoming that turns Voss's journey into a quest, into a myth and makes him part of legends and history. Thus Colonel Hebden says: "Mr. Voss is already history." (413) This makes Voss an ideal being enwrapped by an inscrutable mystery. People are up and about to find out the concrete reality as to Voss's end. Thus Dugald and Boyle question the black fellow to know the truth. The Colonel also goes along with his search but fails. Finally Judd presents the bare truth of his death.

But it does not remain confined to an area of information; rather it becomes part of knowledge: "Perhaps true knowledge only comes of death by future in the country of the mind." Laura comes to visualize the ultimacy of an abstraction, of a man turning into an idea. So she says: "Voss did not die. He is there still . . . and always will be." (448) This rightly affirms the entelechy of the gradualism that develops from 'being' to 'becoming.'

NOTES

1. *Voss* (Penguin Books, 1977), back cover.
2. See R. Graves, *The Greek Myths* (Penguin Books, 1978), p. 100.

Indomitable Spirit of Nautre in Patrick White's *Voss*

V.C. SUDHEER

Patrick White's *Voss* may be analyzed as a study of Man. It is the study of a human being with a strong desire to be 'God' and lead 'ordinary' mortals to salvation but in the process destroyed by Nature and other men. *Voss* is the timeless story of a journey—a voyage to the unknown and the eternal desire of man to conquer Nature and enslave 'evil'—a struggle which goes on for ever. There is an epic character in this novel which sometimes reminds us of Milton and Tolstoy. There is a nobility in the theme and a strength of purpose displayed all through which raises the subject to epic proportions. *Voss* may be termed as a 'human epic' which portrays the power of Man in all his naked glory. The contemporary social scene and colonial backdrop of the novel serves only to give authenticity to the theme but seems to be a world apart from the world of the hero, Voss. To the very end, the strength of his purpose—the strong, motivated desire to reveal the unknown and to face disaster smilingly, never surrendering his power of the will—leaves us astounded.

The novel opens with a meeting of the two main characters Voss and Laura Trevelyan, the niece of Mr. Bonner. He is the sponsor of the expedition led by Voss which is setting forward to discover the vast, unknown expanses of the deserts of the Australian continent for the first time. The story is set in the colonial settlement of Australia. Voss is a German who, fired with the spirit of adventure, comes to take part in the expedition. Laura finds Voss different from all the other men she has met, both in appearance and behaviour. He is rough, uncouth and uncivil compared to the suave polished gentlemen she met in parties and picnics which was almost a daily feature and source of entertainment for her immediate society. But Laura, too, was different. In their later meetings, we discover in Laura a kindred soul—the fiery, bold and adventurous streak in her which lies bound by social norms and the false, frivolous codes of conduct which her aunt Mrs. Bonner seems to epitomize. The love that grows between the two apparently different people is a love between two mentally attuned souls—a bond which can never be broken. The love between Laura and Voss remains an interesting side-theme in the novel but never emphasizes itself. Her silent love gives a character to the aimless wanderings of a madman. *Voss* gets its life-spirit from the feelings of Laura and her unflinching loyalty towards the character of Voss. In the end, Laura meets Judd, one of the survivors of the mission of Voss, and comes to know for certain that Voss is dead. When Judd proclaims that Voss was no 'God' but a true Christian who "was more than a man" (443) who would serve the sick and the distressed, Laura is moved and she agrees with him totally. She tells Colonel Hebden, "I am convinced that Voss had in him a little of Christ, like other men. If he was composed of evil along with the good, he struggled with that evil. And failed." (445) Her immense faith in Voss and her quiet strength of character is evident in these words.

Laura is unconventional both in looks and spirits. She does not impress in the flowery and 'sweet' way that her cousin Belle Bonner or other girls of her age and society do. Here is the beauty of personality. She has the charms of intelligence, wit and mature understanding which men like Tom Radclyffe find a trifle disconcerting. She has the courage and convictions of a man clothed in feminine attributes which is her special appeal. In the frivolous and artificial world of men and women she dares to stand for the 'truth.' She decides to adopt the daughter of Rose Portion, the family servant who had embarrassed the Bonner family by her illegitimate conception. She even contemplates giving up ideas of settling down in order to keep her promise given to the dying Rose. Thus, Laura is great in her self-sacrifice and high ideals. We find the other feminine characters like Mary and Belle Bonner pale in comparison. Both Laura and Voss are incomprehensible to others but mutually well-complimented.

The plot is simple—the story of a tragic expedition undertaken by a few daring men which meets with expected failure. The imaginative tale of the terrible voyage and the inevitable end is etched with the sympathetic eyes of the writer. The story is powerful in its human appeal. The tragic end of Voss at the hands of his trusted black servant Jackie, is intensely powerful. That a white should meet his end at the hands of a black, the native of soil, suggests racial unity though in a subdued way. In the tragic circumstances, where Voss lies waiting for death, the killer is like a merciful Messiah relieving a tormented soul from his body. There is a heavenly aura about this scene which haunts our minds for quite some time. Voss assumes a superhuman form in the course of the novel and elevates it. But there are also personal feelings and common human emotions displayed which makes it a novel. The characters are stark, real and living. Judd is a solid and down-to-earth convict who sees the practical side of the situation and ultimately revolts against Voss. Turner and Angus follow him since they lack a will of their own. Palfreyman is an epitome of goodness. It is perhaps justified that he should give his life for a cause. He strives to bring about peace between the natives and his people and singly braves their spears. He becomes a Christ-like figure by his actions. Frank Le Mesurier too brings about his own end but does not betray Voss. Harry gives his life never leaving the side of Voss. The picture of barren Nature and slow decay of animal life is tragic and vivid. It gives us a glimpse of alien forces of Nature as opposed to human endeavour. Voss is an epic hero who fights against tremendous odds and although a failure by human standards, succeeds in spirit. Indomitable spirit gives him immortality.

The end of the novel poses a question. Who was right—the mutineers who had left for a peaceful existence safe in their homes or the brave fighters who gave their lives to accomplish a 'dream'? Laura's meeting with Judd is a revelation. Judd says although he had left Voss half-way he did not get back to his family since his wife and children had died in his absence. There is an irony in the question, 'who is greater.' Undoubtedly, Voss is the more dignified of the two. He dies a more heroic death. But, as, Laura concludes, "Voss did not die, . . . He is there still, it is said in the country and always will be. His legend will be written down, eventually, by those who have been troubled by it." (448) These words seem to be the declaration of the novelist himself who based his novel on the true record of Ludwig Leichhardt, who died in the Australian desert in 1848.

A New Passage to India: Patrick White's *The Tree of Man*

VERONICA BRADY

Of all Patrick White's works *The Tree of Man,* published in 1953, is perhaps the most in tune with traditional Indian culture. Even more perhaps than most of his other novels, however, it is written out of an urgent personal need, the need to find the "extraordinary within the ordinary," discover some centre for his life beyond the merely material. Having turned his back on Australia in the 1930s after he came down from Cambridge, White had returned to Australia in 1948. After his experiences of war in the African desert and in London during the Blitz, the landscape of Greece which he visited shortly after the War was over had reminded him of the Australian landscape, of the "state of silence, simplicity and humility" it seemed to embody for him as a child and which, disgusted with the empty sophistications of London intellectual life as well as with the moral and physical bankruptcy he felt in post-war Europe in which, he wrote, "the ghosts of Homer, St. Paul and Tolstoy sat waiting for the crash." It was time, he felt, to come home.

But, settled with his friend, Manoly Lascaris, on a small farm at Castle Hill on the outskirts of Sydney, he soon began to be disillusioned. All around him stretched what he called "the Great Australian Ugliness" in which the mind seemed the least of possessions and the spiritual life seemed nonexistence, crushed by the imperatives of making money and consuming and accumulating material possessions. Understandable enough perhaps in a society which had been precipitated from the Great Depression (which had hit Australia (very hard) to the austerities of war, his preoccupation with material things and mindless pleasures was nevertheless peculiarly distasteful to White, who had come home in search of something he felt he had lost within himself, some deep and peaceful centre of self. So he was deeply troubled by what he felt all around him. In writing *The Tree of Man* he attempted to warm himself back to spiritual life, to rediscover the "silence, simplicity and humility" he had experienced as a child in the

Australian countryside.

Since the publication of David Marr's monumental biography, we also know that this novel coincided with the crucial spiritual experience of his life. One rainy day during this time, the early fifties carrying a bucket of slops to feed a litter of pups, he slipped and fell flat on his back in the mud, spilling the slops all over him. Lying there cursing, he suddenly realized that he was cursing a God in whom he had always said he did not believe. From that time onwards, he told David Marr, he became a believer, not, it is true, in the God of conventional religion—he found little sense of divinity there—but in some "mysterioum tremendous, et fascinans," a mysterious presence to be found both within and beyond the self which was both awesome, even terrifying, and yet also utterly compelling and gracious. In one of his later novels, *The Vivisector,* one of the characters, Mrs. Volkhov, compares this experience with the sting of the wasp, painful, yet an experience which rinses one clean, "like a washed plate," empties the self, allowing infinity to flow in.

For all these reasons, therefore, it is not surprising that in Australia *The Tree of Man* had a mixed reception. Most Australians in the 1950s tended to be intent upon prosperity, security and conformity—it was the height of the Cold War. Superficially, as one critic, A.D. Hope, pointed out, the novel seemed to resemble that "mythical Bunyip" or legendary monster, the Great Australian Novel, since it drew on the pioneering legend. Stan and Amy Parker were settlers who went out into the bush to clear a farm for themselves, contending with droughts, floods and bushfires to make a good life for themselves. Moreover, like most men of his generation and like White himself, Stan went away to war on the other side of the world. But the tone of the novel was somehow very different, introspective rather than concerned with external events as traditional "realistic" Australian novels were.

The crucial question, then, is to decide what kind of novel it is. White himself makes this clear when he signalled his rejection of what he called the "dun-coloured realism" which had in his opinion for too long characterized Australian fiction. The pressures which drove him were different, pressures of personal spiritual necessity. For him, as for writers like Joyce and Lawrence whom he admired, writing was less a way of drawing a picture of the world than of making himself within. But this put him at odds with a culture preoccupied with the material, largely unwilling to accept any level of reality beyond the observable world of any meaning or purpose beyond those of the purely human realm. Its gestures tended to be exclusive, to claim certainty according to the law of identity which insists on difference rather than unity, on the logic of "either/or" rather than of "both/and." White's sense of reality, however, was more inclusive and expansive. Truth for him not a matter of definition and control but to be sought, a process of listening and humility and language has less to do with reference than with suggestion and implication, not the clarity of the sign but the complexity and ambiguity of the symbol.

Read in this light, the novel's opening which many readers as well as critics find slow and uninteresting takes on new significance. First of all, there are the echoes of *Genesis*, echoes often noted but not always fully understood since they point to the mythical sense of reality which the language dramatizes, a sense of reality not as hierarchically divided between human beings and the rest of creation, reason and matter if you like, but as one great whole. This, however, is the sense expressed in *Genesis*, 2, 7 in which God is said to have "formed man out of the dust of the ground and breathed life into his nostrils," so that in this way, in being related to the rest of life as well as in sharing God's spirit, "man became a living being." The novel's language echoes this.

In the first paragraph the man, his cart, the horse and the tree, animate and inanimate, seem interchangeable. The description is not literal, less visual than synaesthetic as one level of reality merges into the other. The "hairy" tree becomes a human being and the cart "grazing" the tree and the horse "sighing" are all drawn into the man's intention which is in turn mastered by these larger processes of life. Similarly when, shortly afterwards, Stan lights a fire, illuminating the shapes of the trees, one is reminded of Heidegger's image in which human consciousness is compared to a fire which lights up and thus gives intelligibility to a dark forest.

This notion of reality as essentially symbolic will be comprehensible to any one familiar with traditional Indian culture, of course. It is not a mere matter of allusion here, however, but the key to an understanding of the novel and its purposes as a whole. Its ground in a sense lies ahead of itself—as Paul Ricoeur reminds us, the symbol "gives us to think," is generative, not merely descriptive—drawing the reader to experience what cannot be put into words but must be lived, "what you do not know," i.e. merely rationally, as White himself puts it, "but know" i.e. experience intuitively.

To begin with, the novel's title *The Tree of Man* points in this direction, to the notion of the cosmic tree connecting heaven and earth familiar to traditional Indian culture, as indeed to most mythic systems. But it also echoes the passage in Wordsworth's *The Prelude* (Book VI, 635-40) in which, crossing the Alps, the poet is suddenly aware of the woods, waters, winds and mountains drawn together in some vast and complex unity:

Tumult and peace, the darkness and the light—
Were all like workings of one mind, the features
Of the same face, blossoms upon one tree;
Characters of the great Apocalypse,
The types and symbols of Eternity,
Of first, and last, and midst, and without end. (635-40)

This reference to this part of *The Prelude* also provides an insight into the nature of the novel's action and of the kind of heroism embodied in its two main characters. Stan especially. To underline the rejection of the either/or of identity/difference. This insight into the unity of things follows the anti-climactic moment in which the poet and his friends who had expected that crossing the highest point of the Alps would be dramatic, are told that they have done so without knowing it. They "had hopes that pointed to the clouds." (587) But suddenly a new intuition seizes the poet, one in which passivity becomes more important than action and inaction rather than achievement. It begins with the realization that

. . . I was lost,
Halted without an effort to break through. (596-97)

But out of this realization, this sense of "usurpation" a new understanding begins to emerge:

. . . when the light of sense
Goes out, but with a flash that has revealed
The invisible world, doth greatness make abode. (600-2)

It "harbours" there, in this state of apparent unknowing. In this wise passivity, the soul

Seeks for no trophies, struggles for no spoils
That may attest her prowess, blest in thoughts
That are their own perfection and reward,
Strong in herself and in beatitude
That hides her. (610-14)

What is known is not "practical" but existential, the intuition that

Our destiny, our being's heart and home,
Is with infinitude, and only there. (604-5)

To a culture concerned with material success, achievements and possessions, Stan and Amy Parker who achieve very little are both uninteresting and unimportant. But read in this light, they become significant. Theirs is an interior journey and they are heroes of passivity rather than action and hence the emphasis throughout on their being lead rather than making decisions or initiating projects. On this journey the destiny, their Karma, seems to unfold from within and their task is to go with it and with its rhythms. So the "events" of the novel are not so much things that they do as experiences they endure, moments of insight and intuition, a glimpse of dew on the cabbages in the early morning, for instance, or the storm which blows up after which Amy conceives her first child or Stan's glimpse of the globe shrivelling up at the heart of the burning mansion of Glastonbury, and so on. So it is, too, that the novel's climax comes at the end in the moment in which, an old man poor and very frail, sitting in the garden he made which has now gone to seed, Stan catches a glimpse of the "large triumphal scheme" of things, the series of concentric circles of which he is suddenly aware, his life constitutes a part.

To underline the point that achievement lies in passivity and that the goal of all speech as well as of all action is silence, this understanding is interrupted by the arrival of a brash young evangelist trying to "tell Stan things" about the glories of salvation. In reply, like a Zen master disdaining words and explanations, Stan spits and then, pointing to the gob of spittle "glittering intensely and personally on the ground," says to the young man "that is God." What can be put into words is not what really needs to be put into words. What is ultimately the case exceeds language. As Wittgenstein puts it, "whereof we cannot speak, thereof we must remain silent."

The significant events of the novel, then, are made up of such moments, a series of "showings" or to use Wordsworth's term, "apocalypse" in which what it manifests itself. Indian readers, once again, will be familiar with this notion of manifestation, *pradurbhava.* Similarly, the various travellers who appear from time to time and visit the Parkers' farm can be seen as aviators, visitants from elsewhere. Similarly, characters like Madeleine, Mr. Gage, Bub and Doll Quigley, Con the Greek and Fritz the German manifest various aspects of existence, beautiful or painful, destructive or creative, offering us an insight into the "workings of the one mind, the features of the same face, blossoms upon [the] one tree" of life.

In effect, therefore, *The Tree of Man* interrogates the epistemological and ontological foundations of culture, its confidence in matter-of-fact and what it calls commonsense. This is another reason, of course, for the problems it caused and continues to cause many readers and critics. But Indian readers will be aware that it belongs within another and larger tradition of thought, what we may broadly call mythical or symbolic thinking—something with which most Indians are familiar. In this mode neither the objects of the external world nor human actions, properly speaking, have any intrinsic value. They only acquire value and in so doing become "real" by their participation in a reality which transcends them. An object, even one as apparently unimportant as the little nutmeg grater Amy finds, for instance, or the dew on a cabbage, can become a receptacle of the force of this reality which sets it apart from its external milieu and gives it meaning and value. This meaning and value depends on its ability to reproduce or reflect some primordial action, the fire echoed in the piece of glass the child saved from the flood given Amy, for example. In this sense "reality" derives from the imitation of celestial archetypes.

None of this is to deny the novelist's very real ability to describe actual people and situations. White's observation of characters like Stan's friend Ossie Peabody, laconic, suspicious and emotionally defensive, is shrewd and accurate. So are his descriptions of Ray's youthful cruelties, Thelma's pretentious gentility, the sufferings of Fritz the German and the transformation of Con the Greek from handsome youth to fat and prosperous fish-shop proprietor. Similarly, for all the apparent exaggeration, the O'Dowds are recognizable types. The point is, however, that all these characters play out their lives against this larger backdrop and that their imposition is metaphorical as well as literal. The aim of literal language is in the long run to convince us that the observable world is the only one. But the way in which character and event here become polysemous, part of a larger search for meaning of human existence and of contemporary history, enlarges our understanding, suggesting a notion of relationship rather than mere individuality.

In this way the various events of the novel, the flood, the fire, the drought, the war and its cruelties become part of a larger chain of implication, a testing of the various possibilities of experience. So it is possible to lick Thelma's impression of the city at night (251) with the "showing" of the fire at Glastonbury in which Stan's illusions about the splendours of the house and the seductive beauty of Madeleine are consumed by fire from which Madeleine emerges, her splendid head of hair burnt off, a pitiable creature crawling on all fours from the ruin of the house, an image of the "naked unaccommodated thing itself." Similarly, the motif of the tree which links heaven and earth recurs throughout, concluding the novel as it opens it "so that in the end there was no end." In this way inner and outer reality are interwoven and determinations of identity are broken apart by the inbreaking of alterity, manifestations of some further reality beyond the appearances.

Both Stan and to a lesser extent, Amy, live towards and by this reality so that as we have said, there is a strange passivity about their lives. They do not so much choose to do or suffer this or that but are chosen: "All things happen that are intended," (148) as the narrator remarks. This is true also of characters like the Quigleys, Bub and Doll and Mr. Gage who also live as it were across boundaries, refusing to be possessive, even of themselves or their purposes. But for this reason, they are "singularly free" (195); they possess a special kind of wisdom, the kind Stan's grandson describes when he asks, "Don't you even know, Grandpa, about things you just know?" (393) This kind of knowledge makes them solitary because it is essentially incommunicable. But it also makes them strong because it releases them from the need to give deference to fashion or convention. Coming to the city from their farm, Stan and Amy do not "go down before the anonymous waves (of faces in the street). They discovered they were strong. Their solitary lives had perhaps built them buttresses." (399)

Obviously, this takes them and their purposes in the opposite direction to that of the protagonists of the conventional novel, oriented as it is towards marriage, money, social achievement and heroic action. The key to understanding *The Tree of Man* lies elsewhere in other literary references, to Blake and Pound but especially to Hamlet. The references to Hamlet culminate in the scene near the end of the novel in which Stan and Amy go to see the play during their last visit to the city and this scene, in effect, constitutes the Australian recognition scene. Watching the play they recognize themselves, Amy is the "rather thin woman," Ophelia, who finally drops out of the play, and Stan is Hamlet, though for him, Ophelia is Madeleine, the woman who betrays him. As he also realizes, the play "is too complicated to follow unless lived" (405) and what it finally has to tell him is that he is about to die.

The intertextual reference, that is to say, is placed in the syntax of life lived in a context larger than that of society, lived towards death, which displaces matter-of-fact with its weight. Stan thus discovers himself here as Heidegger's Daisein, the point at which being (Sein) is conscious of itself as being there (da). This discovery is implicit in the opening scene in which, having stopped his cart to make camp for the night, Stan lights a fire echoing a Heidegger's image of consciousness as the equivalent of a fire lit in a dark forest which lights up and gives recognizable shape to what has hitherto been concealed in the darkness. But the identification with Hamlet also adds a new weight of Care (Sorge) to the intuition which gives a new poignancy to Stan's situation.

As Heidegger describes it, there are three elements, three temporal modes to Care. First of all, as here, it involves a concern for what is to be, for futurity, in this case Stan's death. But the awareness of being vulnerable, being-towards-death, also points back to the past, being thrown into existence. Finally there is the awareness of being at this particular moment in time and history, being with this situation, these people, this moment of history. In this way, drawing together past, present and future the moment of care prepares us for the moment in which Stan will understand finally that "One and no other number is the answer to all sums."

This, then, is the sense of reality the novel develops as it were philosophically. But this development depends also upon the novel's design, the web of relationships it weaves between people and the world around them. Animate and inanimate, the elements, colours, textures, images, sounds, the rhythm of the narration as well as its division into the four seasons, spring, summer, autumn and winter. This, of course, is the unity, the series of concern recircles gravely revolving "around him" which Stan glimpses sitting in his wintry and now shabby garden just before he dies. But he is only able to glimpse it because he has surrendered all claims to domination and possession and allowed himself to be taken up into the "large, triumphal scheme."

Significantly, therefore, the novel begins in springtime but ends in winter. As he puts it in his first published story, "The Twitching Colonel," White believes that "it is only in dissolution [that we find] salvation." At the beginning Stan sets out into the wilderness to tame it and turn it into a farm and a garden. But here at the end of it the processes of decay, decreation, which seems to have prevailed over those of creation. His garden has gone to seed, Stan himself has had a stroke and his body is increasingly frail and helpless and winter has set in. In terms of commonsense these are images of failure and defeat. Instead of transforming the energies of the natural world, turning natura naturans into natura naturata by shaping it to his own ends, Stan is increasingly subject to its power, physical necessity.

Yet this, the novel implies, is the way of wisdom; submission rather than the Promethean rebellion the determination to subject the natural world to the imperatives of the human will characteristic of Western civilization today. As a child, White tells us in his autobiography *Flaws in the Glass,* his favourite places were those in which he could celebrate these mysteries of decreation, places in the family garden in which he became aware of the processes of decay like a pile of mouldering autumn leaves, pools so cold that they took your breath away or crags in the Blue Mountains where the rocks seemed about to crack apart.

Indian culture knows about Siva the destroyer as well as the creator and Kali goddess of dark destructive powers. White echoes these intuitions throughout *The Tree of Man* but especially at the end when Stan's intuition of the "large triumphal scheme" is torn apart by the arrival of the young evangelist. He is determined to tell Stan things about God and about the "salvation" he is selling as if it were just another commodity. But Stan knows that what ultimately matters, what is ultimately worshipful is a matter of absence rather than presence and cannot be put into words, that the only way to wisdom is to destroy commonsense, even profane it.

In this way the novel rejects the way of conscious intentionality in order to display a larger pattern of existence into which the individual life is subsumed, not, however, to be negated but to be fulfilled. Hindu and, to a lesser extent, Buddhist thought is comfortable with this intuition. But so, too, is the mystical tradition of Christianity, as of all great religions. Eliot's *Four Quartets,* for instance, turn on it. Stan's experience here and as he moves towards death at the end of *The Tree of Man* echoes this moment in "Little Gidding," for instance:

> We move above the moving tree
> In light upon the figured leaf
> And bear upon the sodden floor
> Below, the boar hound and the boar
> Pursue their pattern as before
> But reconciled among the stars.

Most of us, like the young evangelist and most of the other characters in the novel, may have "the experience but miss the meaning," as Eliot puts it. The meaning is summed up also in *Four Quartets,* and embodied in the story of Stan Parker:

> The only wisdom we can hope to acquire
> Is the wisdom of humility: humility is endless.

which no doubt is why the novel concludes that "in the end there was no end."

The Tree of Man thus has profound implications for an increase in understanding between Australian and Indian culture. Since the Enlightenment, Western culture has tended to make the human mind the measure of all reality and rationality the norm, regarding ourselves as superior to other cultures which allow room also for the intuitive and the mythical. So Henry Kissinger could write condescendingly that "empirical reality has a much different significance for many of the new countries (and he would undoubtedly include India here, newness being a matter of Western perception rather than of history) than for the West because in a certain sense they never went through the process of discovering it." The West, as he goes on to argue, has become "committed to the notion that the real world is external to the observer [and] that knowledge consists in recording and classifying data." In *The Tree of Man,* however, Patrick White takes us away from this binary division between self and world, a division whose effects are now becoming apparent in the environmental crisis, for example in the direction of an older, unitary sense of existence, invoking fable and myth to heal the tragic wounds of history which underlie the story of Stan and Amy Parker as of so many ordinary people throughout the world.

The circular shape of *The Tree of Man* is not accidental. The notion of history as linear, moving towards a future which is always better than the past—what is new is ipso facto better than what is not—has given rise to the notions of "progress" and "development" which until recently have tended to govern public policy and private endeavour in Australia, as in most Western societies. But White sets the lives of his characters within a circle, the larger cycles of existence, birth and death, the seasons and the rhythms of planets and stars, as well as of the great archetypes which recur in human consciousness and are bodied forth in myth and in literature. Superficially, Stan seems a typical pioneer, someone who settles in and opens up a new country, turning the wilderness into "civilization." But, as we have been arguing, what matters rather is that at the deeper level he finally comes to discover "the still point of the turning wheel" of history, the point of deep intuitive consciousness, the archaic knowledge of myth, of the world as ultimately holy because it becomes a place in which Being reveals itself, Awe, not mastery, is the goal. What Stan discovers is as Wittgenstein puts it, the ultimate mystery is not why things are but that they are.

I would argue that these are important insights for Australian culture and society as well as for Indian readers. They also raise important questions about the worth of literature and the act of reading itself, recalling us to the task of interpretation not as an attempt to match words with things and the appearance of things but, as Derrida would have it, as an endless task of deferral, of moving away into further implication, the ploy of language and the syntax of myths and dreams. But these are matters to be taken up on another occasion. For the moment my argument has been that *The Tree of Man* opens the way to a deeper rapprochement between Australia and India.

Australian Short Fiction: The Last Thirty Years

PRADEEP TRIKHA

It was in 1968, that the editor of *Australian Letters*, Geoffery Dutton, remarked, "Writing verse and short stories must be the greatest underground activity in Australia."[1] In the following decade short story regained a prominent position in Australian literature. In the brief history of Australian short story one finds four phases, (I) "The Colonial Phase" (1788-1890) in which the themes were sensational, (II) the second from 1890s to 1950s in which Henry Lawson gave new direction by writing stories of "bush realism," (III) the third phase lasted from 1940 to 1970 during which Australian society experienced transition. (IV) It is only in the fourth phase beginning in the 70s that contemporary Australian short story has come to prominence. The writers of this phase are preoccupied with "a high degree of self awareness, a deep seated sceptism, about what constitutes 'reality' in human affairs."[2] The contemporary writers are Alan Marshall, John Morrison, Peter Cowan, Xavier Herbert, Hal Porter, Dal Stivens, Thelma Forshaw, Peter Carey, Murray Bail, Morris Lurie, Robert Dawe, Michael Wilding and Frank Moorhouse.

The bulk of their works reinforced Australian identity in the international short story scene. Like their predecessors Lawson and Furphy, they too felt that the art of "short story is indigenous to Australia" and that "the short story was an ideal medium to highlight the infinite variety of character, viewpoint, occupation, incident and mood that made up the whole"[3] but unlike Lawson and Furphy, these writers have set examples which are new and different, like Judith Wright in poetry and Patrick White in the novel they craved to redefine Australia. This is also the concern to be found in playwrights like David Williamson, Dorothy Hewett and filmmakers like Tom Burstall and Michael Thornhill. This new iconography is largely based on their experience of Australian urban reality.

Writers like Moorhouse, Wilding and Carey feel that the short story is more flexible and open form to experiment than the novel and this form is more adaptable to their audience. These writers achieved a break-through in representing experiences which are different from their predecessors. They experimented with the form and "were stimulated by the resurgent radicalism of the anti-Vietnam protest, the influence of contemporary American . . . writing."[4] Also there was widespread use of drugs and resentment against prohibited literature and the Federal Government. Moorhouse commented once, "The great need in Australian short story writing is still that it should go too far and resist blandness."[5] In fact the writers are expected to question the conventional ways of telling a story. In this process Wilding in *Tabloid Story Pocket Book* observes, "what we rejected were the false uses of the Lawson tradition and dubious nationalism." Their stories are a reflection of contemporary culture and politics. Moorhouse feels that the art of story telling in Australia "is the art of living in Australia." He emphasizes, "it is something of a map of social concerns, are a part of background."[6] There is a close connection between Wilding and Moorhouse's stories and Australian society, they are multiculturally aware, are nationalists but not chauvinists. They are hottest literary property. They have been billed as "clever, intelligent, shrewd and exciting in one way or another."[7]

Issues like sex and male understanding of sex are dealt by both of them. They concentrate on the 'complexities' of the issues while Wilding writes about 'superficialities.' Both authors share common environment, friends, activities and interests. Thus at times, their materials in short fiction are similar, but with radical difference of opinions. Fryar points out why Moorhouse is a better craftsman: "Wilding lacks the sense of self criticism which Moorhouse uses to reveal the futility and comedy of life. Moorhouse and Wilding with few other writers persisted with schemes to advance short fiction, activities which were themselves sometimes fictionalized. Moorhouse's 'discontinuous narrative,' and books like Wilding's *Short Story Embassy: A Novel* and *Scenic Drive* or Christine Townand's *Travel with Myself* e.g. were made possible in the new situation. By the end of 70s fruits of the change emerged with the success of the books like *The Americans, Baby, The Electrical Experience* and *The Fat Man in History* amongst a number of others. Their short stories record the 'counter culture' of Australia in the sense Michael Lerner elaborates: "norms and patterns of behaviour of emerging institutions (such as rock festivals and communes) and beliefs and artistic traditions that have coalesced to provide an opposing alternative to the cultural templates of the main culture. It is a term broadly applied to radical students, hippies, motorcycle gangs, the homosexual Gay Power movement, Women's Liberation groups. . . . The core of the counter culture is the sector which carries through most completely the transvaluation of values. . . . Many of the counter culture's characteristics . . . wish to reject completely the main culture."[8] Moorhouse and Wilding have established "an intellectual and situational framework in which the issues of insecurity, sexual and other relationships can be examined." (Fryar)

Peter Carey, Murray Bail, Morris Lurie and Robert Dawe belong to the tribe of Moorhouse and Wilding. Like them they too are disenchanted with the worn-out set of values and conventions which had dominated the Australian short story for about a century or so. Peter Carey is one of the most popular and widely admired writers. Moorhouse in his introduction to the 1973 *Coast to Coast* suggested that the short story is "akin to the dream, the oral tale and a fantasy." Carey's two major collections are *The Fat Man in History* and *War Crimes,* his perceptions of contemporary culture, and policies are reflected in his stories. On the other hand Lurie is a traveller at heart, as one of the critics puts it, he is a "culturally conscious tourist." His collections *Running Nicely* and *Dirty Friends* show that "his wit is based on a very serious interest in the way societies discriminate between each other, and the way in which individuals can identify and use the nuances by which those discriminations are made." (Heseltine) Lurie has added memorable comic characters to Australian fiction but with all seriousness.

Like his fellow writers, Bail in his writings gives bleak view of personal relationships. His novel *Homecoming* justifies need for an accounting with one's native land. Robert Dawe's *The Body Surfers*, gives quintessential Australian experiences. Other than these writers Barry Oakley, Barry Hill and John Emrey also came into prominence during the later 70s and 80s. They rediscovered stories of city life. Their stories depicted the cities and the young, e.g. Oakley's *Walking through Tiger Land* depicts stories of city life. Hill's evocation of an outer suburban waste-land in *A Rim of Blue* or Emrey's *Summer Ends Now* in no way involve radical shifts in mode.

These writers are eager to modulate out of the mimetic mode at those points where their fictions probe the limits of ordinary experience. In general, however, the expansion in short fiction during the last decade has been notable for the numerous stories which extend or simply ignore, the conventions of realism associated with novel. They recover some of the potential inherent in the tale in its various literary and oral forms, and exploit the verbal and formal possibilities of brevity and compressions. Altogether there has been a shift from the representational to the *inventive* capacity of fiction.[9]

One of the most interesting innovations in the recent Australian short fiction is Moorhouse's 'discontinuous narrative.' Not only in themes but also in his techniques of writing he reveals remarkable maturity. Moorhouse has a fine control over dialogue and complexity of tone. His structural method of narration which he defines as 'discontinuous' one, has long flowing sentences, interrelates with each other at the end. The style is impressionistic and narrative gripping. It was with his *The Americans, Baby* that the nature of his 'discontinuous narrative' style became well known. Elaborating his method, Moorhouse says, "These are interlinked stories and although the narrative is discontinuous there is no single plot—the environment and characters are continuous. In some ways people in the story are a tribe." Moorhouse finds 'objective correlative' of his social environment in his discontinuous narratives. His character T. George McDowell, came to us in 'fragments' but these fragments have structural links. In an interview in *The National Times* he speaks of how the discontinuous narrative is a logical extension of his view of life. He feels, "I don't see any underlying harmony or unity in life."

Peter Carey, Frank Moorhouse, Michael Wilding and few others are widely read authors in Australia today and the themes, settings, characters and the situations of their stories appeal to one and all. In the late 80s and early 90s they published several volumes of short stories and quiet a good number of anthologies all of which attest to their revitalized interest in the Australian short story. They have added notably to the tradition of Australian fiction by rehabilitating the short story and widening its avenues so as to capture areas of contemporary culture in the society. They feel that short fiction is a vital and vibrant cultural vehicle. Thea Astley, Barry Hill, Peter Murphy, John Emrey and James McQueen are still enlarging upon the work of the last two decades. They give the short fiction its distinctly tantalizing quality and we can immediately recognize how their varied experiences form background of their stories.

NOTES

1. Geoffery Dutton and Max Marris, ed., *The Vital Decade* (Melbourne: Penguin, 1963), p. 8.
2. H.P. Heseltine, "Thirty years of Australian Short Story," *Rajasthan University Studies in English*, XV (1982-83), pp. 33-41.
3. Henrietta Drake Brockman, "The International Symposium on the Short Stories," *Kenyon Review*, Vol. 20, No. 4 (1968), pp. 443-90.

4. Ian Turner, "Introduction," *The Literature of Australia*, ed. Geoffrey Dutton (Ringwood: Penguin, 1964), p. 50.
5. Frank Moorhouse, ed., *The State of the Art* (Ringwood: Penguin, 1973), p. 5.
6. *Ibid*, p. 7
7. Miche'le Fryar, "Moorhouse and Wilding as Fiction Writers: Our Hottest Property," *Aspects of Australian Culture*, ed. Joost Daalder and Miche'le Fryar (Melbourne: Oxford University Press, 1986), p. 235
8. "Anarchism and Counter Culture," *Anarchism Today*, ed. D.E. Apter and James Joll (London: Macmillan, 1971), p. 37.
9. Bruce Clunics Ross, "Some Developments in Short Fiction, 1969-1980," *Australian Literary Studies,* Vol. X, No. 2, Oct. 1984, pp. 165-80.

Sense of Place in the Short Stories of Barbara Baynton

C.L.L. JAYAPRADA

Barbara Baynton contributed in a significant manner to the Bush Realism of the eighteen nineties in the Australian literature through her short stories though her general output was not much. Until recently the achievement of the Bush Realism of eighteen nineties brought only the names of short story writers like Henry Lawson, novelists like Joseph Furphy, and poets like Banjo Paterson to one's mind. And the comment of John Barnes is typical of the critical approaches to the output of the period: "Lawson and Furphy stand out from their contemporaries by the authenticity of their bush manner. The rest of the Bulletin story-tellers tend to be local colorists, of varying competence, whose work is superior to that of their Anglo-Australian contemporaries, because they are closer to local ways of feeling and seeing. At best they seem capable of only fragmentary insights."[1] The stories of Barbara Baynton have not received much critical attention and her graphic tales of bush which bring out the savagery and tragedy of the lives closely allied to the land are dismissed as the ones merely containing local colouring.

In Baynton's stories the bush is not merely evoked in all its impressive detail as a background to the stories but it controls and defines the very lives of the central characters. The bush is a home they struggle (battle) to make habitable, a hellish hole which could slowly and savagely erode their sense of security and identity. The bush also becomes a point of self-reference and self-definition for the solitary men and women of Barbara Baynton. It turns her men savagely cunning and her women into alienated and dehumanized figures. The various aspects of the sense of place compounded with her mastery of technique and clinical style make the stories devastatingly powerful. The paper proposes to study the sense of place in the tales of bush by Barbara Baynton.

By the time of her death Barbara Baynton was known to the world as Lady Headley, wife of an English lord famous for her collection of

China and antique furniture. It is difficult to associate such a glamorous lady with the literary world and the vivid depiction of the lives of the lone battlers in the bush unless one looked into her early life. She was the seventh child of a carpenter, worked as a governess and married a selector who deserted her after the birth of three children. She moved to Sydney and struggled to support herself and her children until she met a wealthy seventy-year-old doctor and got married to him. Life with Dr. Baynton gave her necessary leisure and ease to indulge in a calling close to her heart. She began to write living in luxurious surroundings amidst exquisite China and beautiful antique furniture but the early struggle for survival and the compromises she had to make in life compelled her to reject the romance and to choose the realistic and ironic mode. She lived graciously encircled by the significant personalities of time but her pen drew on the bizarre experiences in the immense and grotesque landscape. She stands apart from the women writers of the period Tasma, Mrs. Campbell Praed and Ada Cambridge who portrayed the middle-class life in a sentimental and romantic manner. She shares some of the concerns with Lawson, Furphy and Paterson in the presentation of the lives of the workman in the outback, the use of vernacular diction and rhythms and in the depiction of comedy and absurdity of life shaped by the dictates of the land but her predominant concerns are different from those of the literature of the 1890s for "There is no nationalistic pride, no love of the bush and no feeling of mateship or affinity between the bush and its inhabitants."[2]

Baynton's familiarity with the bush life is intimate and her unparalleled skill in the evocation of place and its ethos is evident in "The Bush Church." The black comedy of the story comes out of the collision of different definitions of the place and the dependent socio-cultural value systems. Lawson and Furphy extol the values of mateship in the bush but Baynton ironically undercuts such celebration and her grip over the ethos is seen in the beginning of the story: "The hospitality of the bush never extends to the loan of a good horse to an inexperienced rider."[3] Thus the Parson bumping along on an old horse, trying to gather people for his service is an incongruous figure for women and children. He has the zeal to reform "the innocent and unlettered brutes" of the bush. But the outback has set its own patterns of thought and behaviour on these victims of raw society which contrast drastically with the parson's expectations. While the service goes on, the men, hoaxed by Ned into believing that the parson is a sneaking Inspector, stick to their seats; the women keep waiting for the food that might be served by the grazier's wife at the end of the service; and the children sneak into the house and gobble up all the food laid on the table for the parson. Only the grazier's wife who is afraid that the parson may take her for one of the bush folk and Alick's old father who had an idea of what the church service might be from the days before he left the old country keep the appearance of reverence during the service. The comedy here ensues from the collision of expectations of people from different places. The savagery of bush life in which getting the bare necessities of life becomes the priority is emphasized and in contrast the utter valuelessness of the religious efforts of the Parson, with his limited understanding is dramatized. Similar clash of expectations of the bush men and the new chum turns "Toohey's Party" into a farce. The determined efforts of the snobbish Anty Jo to keep the party a decent affair by keeping Mrs. Toohey's poor relatives out and the desperate struggle of Mrs. Toohey's young brothers to get in aided by their fierce protector Granny leave Mrs. Toohey in tears.

Baynton is keenly aware not only of the physical effects of the bush on men but also the emotional and spiritual effects. Her intuitive grasp of character is seen in the delineation of the women protagonists of "The Chosen Vessel" and "Billy Skywonkie." These women belong to town originally. For them, the desolation of the barren plains, the "tireless, greedy sun" (47) during the day, the bush noises and the great quavering shadows during the moonlight are terrifying because there is always the unknown danger lurking in them. They find the bush inimical to their sense of security and identity and they identify the bush with the strange predatory men with "the cruel eyes, lascivious mouth and gleaming knife" (84) and together they remind the women of their own defencelessness and sexual vulnerability. In "Billy Skywonkie" the grotesque creature peers closely into the face of the woman in the cart being taken to the homestead: "Never had she seen anything so grotesquely monkeyish. And the nose of this little hairy horror, as he slewed his neck to look into her face, blotted the landscape and dwarfed all perspective."[4] For him she is only an object of sex and to her dismay as his ugly face blots out the vision, his face and the land become one. Her horror reaches a crescendo as she travels further into the land full of emaciated cattle, sheep deadened by heat, dying fowls and she also encounters the leering men who use lurid language and the drunken and jealous women. She reaches the homestead. When she is rejected by the boss for the housekeeper's job because she is not young and is half-Chinese as he has expected "a young piece," her alienation is complete.

The woman in "The Chosen Vessel" lives with her baby in the nightmarish isolation of the bush while her man is away. Her forebodings come true when a swagie attacks her one night. When all her efforts to protect herself in her own home prove futile, she runs out, carrying her baby, to the horseman calling out for help. But the man overburdened with religious guilt and superstition finds the vision of a woman in flowing robes with a child terrifying and flees away. The swagie throttles the woman without actually fulfilling his passion and is left shattered. Baynton's irony is devastating. When "the chosen vessel" Peter falls at the feet of Madonna and cries out with joy "And Hast Thou Chosen me?" the priest accuses him of not saving the woman and the child. In the life in bush the religion is distorted and for the woman who struggled to make a home out of it, the bush proves a mighty enemy.

In "A Dreamer" the pregnant woman returns to her bush home to see her mother after a lapse of years. As she trudges home alone through the storm-ridden night, the bush becomes a home which evokes the childhood memories, it becomes a powerful enemy she fights with, and it also gives her the scope for reflection and reconsideration of her life. She fights fiercely with the raging elements as she wades through the creek in flood. When she almost loses grip over herself the memory of her grey-haired mother, the coming of her child and her husband's love give her strength to fight it through. As she arrives at the house of her dead mother, she also arrives at a self-definition.

In "Squeaker's Mate" for the woman and to some extent to the old man in "Scrammy 'And," the land, the cattle and the sheep are the dearest in life; they protect and nourish these like their very life. There is a complete self-identification with the land but the hostile land after all takes its human toll. Both of them have only their dogs for their mates, they stand unflinching beside the crippled or dying human figures. Scrammy 'And attacks the old man in the night as he has feared. The man dies a lonely death in his bed with wide open eyes as if he is still keeping a watch on the sheep. Scrammy 'And attacks the old man in the night as he has feared. The man dies a lonely death in his bed with wide open eyes as if he is still keeping a watch on the sheep. Scrammy 'And who plans the attack on the old man meticulously is shocked when he finally gets into the hut and flees away forgetting all about the old man's hoard. The bush offers only frustration and horror to this marauder too as it does to the swagie in "The Chosen Vessel." The final ending of the story offers the desolate image of dead man and his rib-broken dog fighting the flies to protect him. The bush is after all the unchallenged master and the marauder even if he is a benign one pays dearly. In "Squeaker's Mate" the nameless woman protagonist saddled with a selfish man toils all her life to bring the land to fruition. Her back is broken when a branch falls on her as she fells the tree and she is crippled for life. His cruel neglect of her needs does not pain her as much as the sight of the thirsty bleating sheep and the neglected land. He brings a new woman from the town. She mutely watches and endures as he sells the sheep and prepares to sell the land. As the new woman tries to steal the water from the bedside of the crippled woman, the dog catches her in a steely grip. While he tries to save her, he becomes the victim of the dog. He reveals his true colours by pleading with her to make the dog leave him and attack his new mate. There is no value for human bonds in this bizarre world. The back-broken woman lying crippled in her bed in silent anger becomes the very symbol of the mute endurance of the land itself.

Thus Baynton has a deeper engagement with the place than that of mere description. Her depiction of bush life in slow and steady strokes with increasing horror, her creation of a nightmarish world bordering on the supernatural remind one of Poe's magnificent evocative power as a story-teller. Yet her grip on the reality is unparalleled, the narration of the way Scrammy 'And manipulates his way to the hut by unpenning the sheep and the description of the way the woman wades through the creek in flood could have been done only by a masterly hand with intimate knowledge of bush.

NOTES

1. John Barnes, "Australian Fiction to 1920," *The Literature of Australia,* ed. Geoffrey Dutton (Harmondsworth: Penguin, 1964), p. 178.
2. Sally Krimmer and Alan Lawson, *Barbara Baynton*, Portable Australian Authors (St. Lucia: University of Queensland Press, 1980), p. ix.
3. *Ibid.*, p. 61.
4. *Ibid.*, p. 50.

Contributors

Madhumalati Adhikari, Rani Durgavati University, Jabalpur
D.N. Bandyopadhyay, University of Burdwan
Urbashi Barat, Rani Durgavati University, Jabalpur
T. Bharathi, S.P. Mahila Visvavidyalayam, Tirupati
Veronica Brady, University of Western Australia, Perth
Madhuri Chatterjee, University of Rajasthan, Jaipur
Suchitra Choudhary, C.V.S., University of Delhi
R.K. Dhawan, S.B.S.C., University of Delhi
M.D. Fletcher, University of Queensland, Australia
C.L.L. Jayaprada, Andhra University, Visakhapatnam
Rosemary Kerr, Victoria, Australia
A.G. Khan, Vikram University, Ujjain
John McLaren, Victoria University of Tech., Melbourne
K. Radha, Kerala University, Trivandrum
Shaik Samad, Shivaji Arts, Com. & Sc. College, Kannad
Ron Shapiro, University of Western Australia, Perth
Anurag Sharma, Dayanand College, Ajmer
Vinod Bala Sharma, University of Delhi
V.C. Sudheer, Andhra University, Visakhapatnam
Pradeep Trikha, Dayanand College, Ajmer

Index